GRAB LIFE BY THE BALLS

And Other Life Lessons from
THE GOOD ADVICE CUPCAKE

LORYN BRANTZ and KYRA KUPETSKY

RUNNING PRESS

PHILADELPHIA

Running Press
Hachette Book Group
1290 Avenue of the Americas, New York, NY 10104
www.runningpress.com
@Running_Press

Printed in China

First Edition: October 2019

Published by Running Press, an imprint of Perseus Books, LLC, a subsidiary of Hachette Book Group, Inc. The Running Press name and logo is a trademark of the Hachette Book Group.

The Hachette Speakers Bureau provides a wide range of authors for speaking events. To find out more, go to www.hachettespeakersbureau.com or call (866) 376-6591.

The publisher is not responsible for websites (or their content) that are not owned by the publisher.

Print book cover design by Susan Van Horn.
Interior design by Loryn Brantz and Kyra Kupetsky.

Library of Congress Control Number: 2019930828

ISBNs: 978-0-7624-6816-4 (hardcover), 978-0-7624-6815-7 (ebook)

1010

10 9 8 7 6 5 4 3 2 1

CONTENTS

CAREER: DRESS FOR SUCCESS

IT IS EXTREMELY IMPORTANT WHEN SEARCHING FOR A JOB TO DRESS FOR SUCCESS!

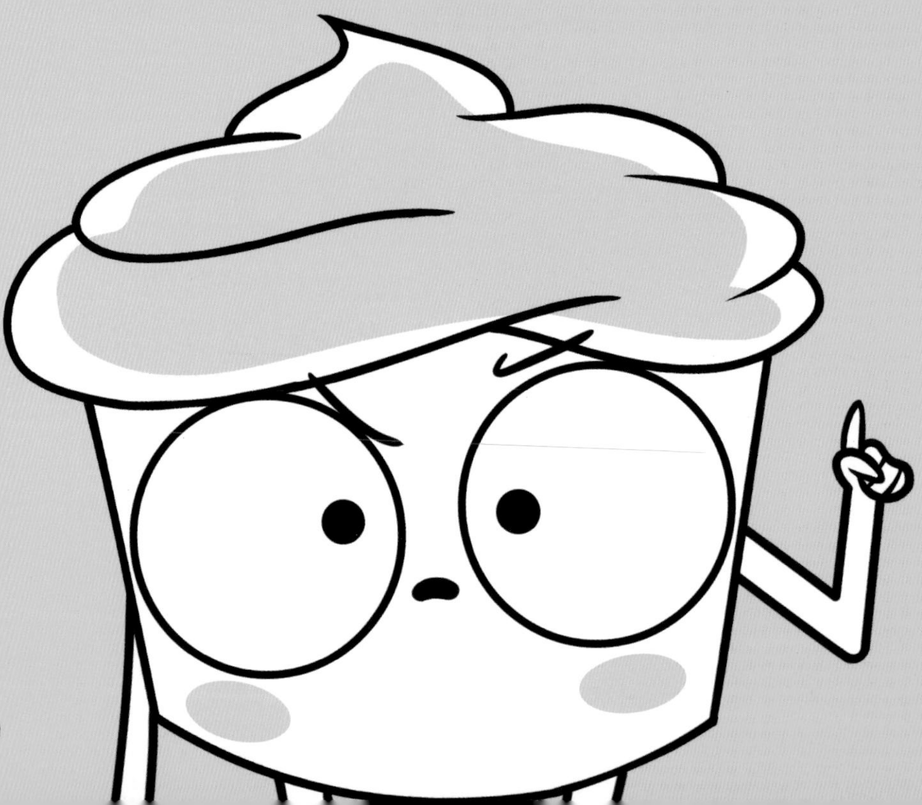

YOU SHOULD DRESS FOR THE JOB YOU WANT, NOT THE JOB YOU HAVE.

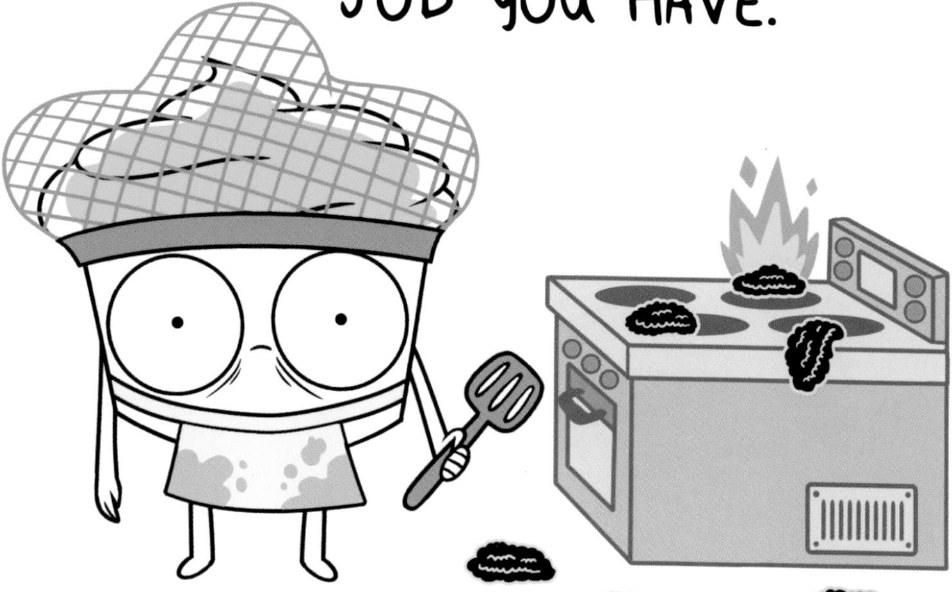

FOR EXAMPLE,
WHILE JOB HUNTING
I ALWAYS WEAR...

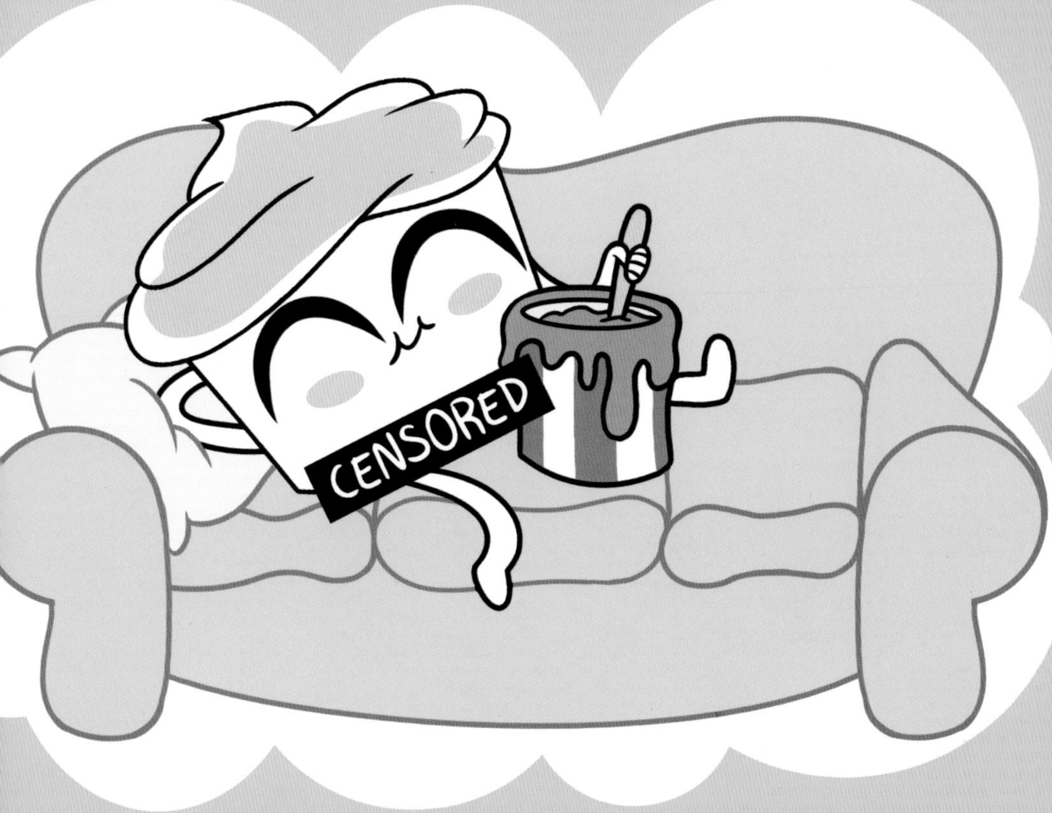
CENSORED

A PROFESSIONAL COUCH RESTER
AND ICE CREAM TASTER!

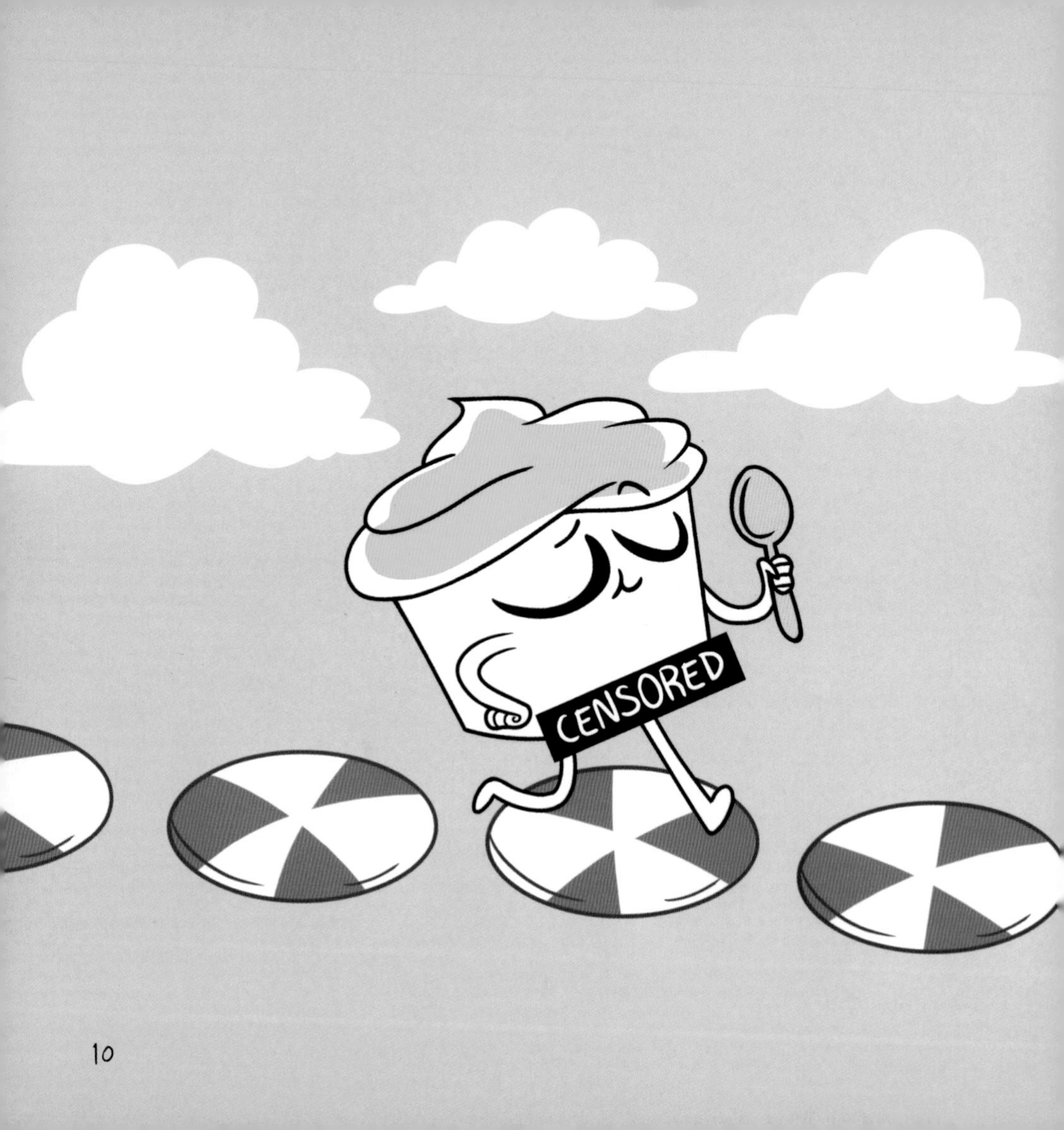
CENSORED

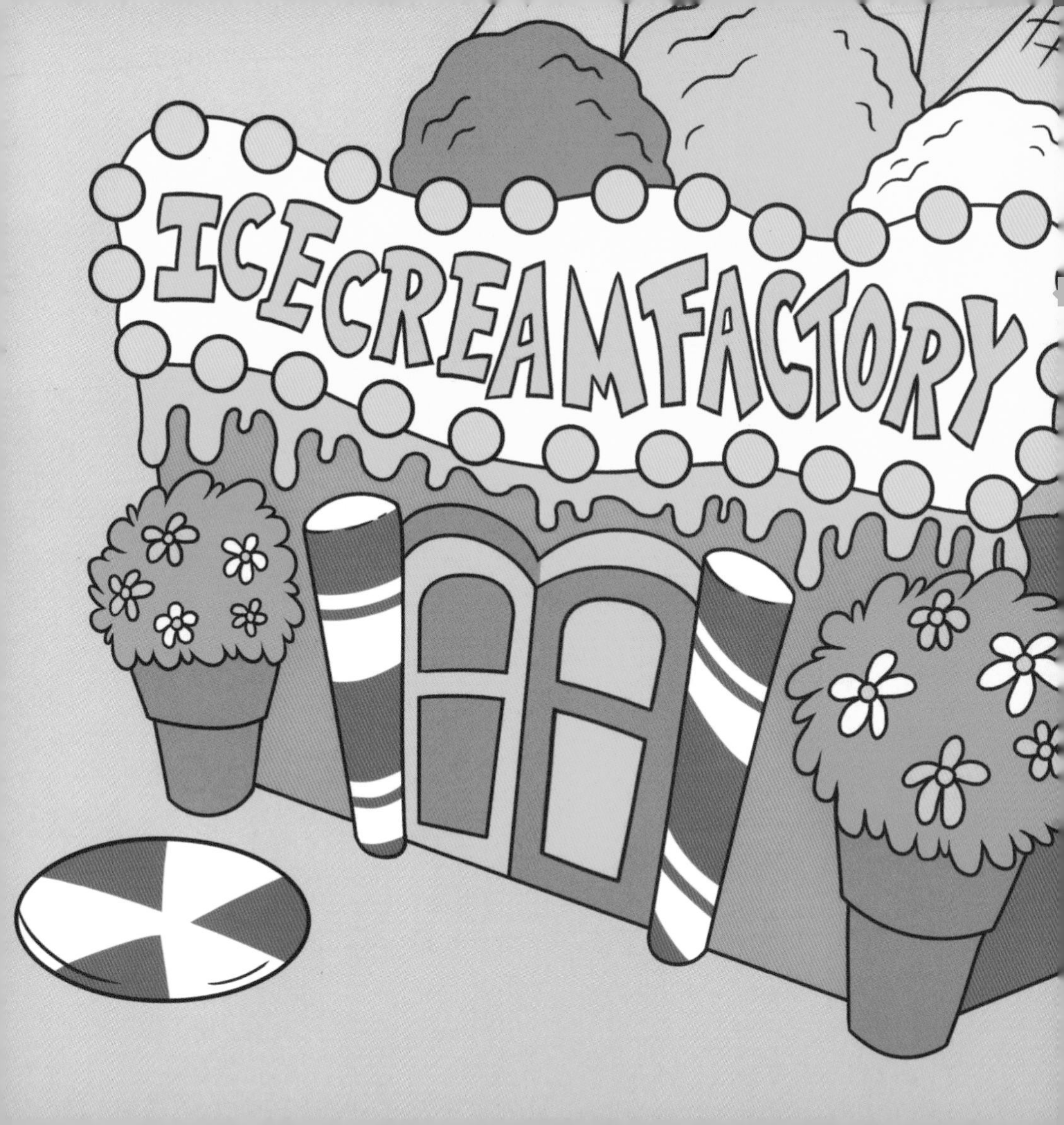
ICE CREAM FACTORY

I'M HERE
FOR THE...

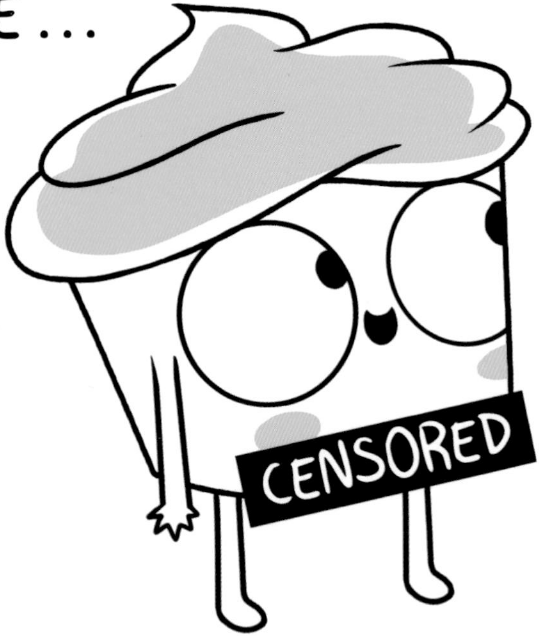

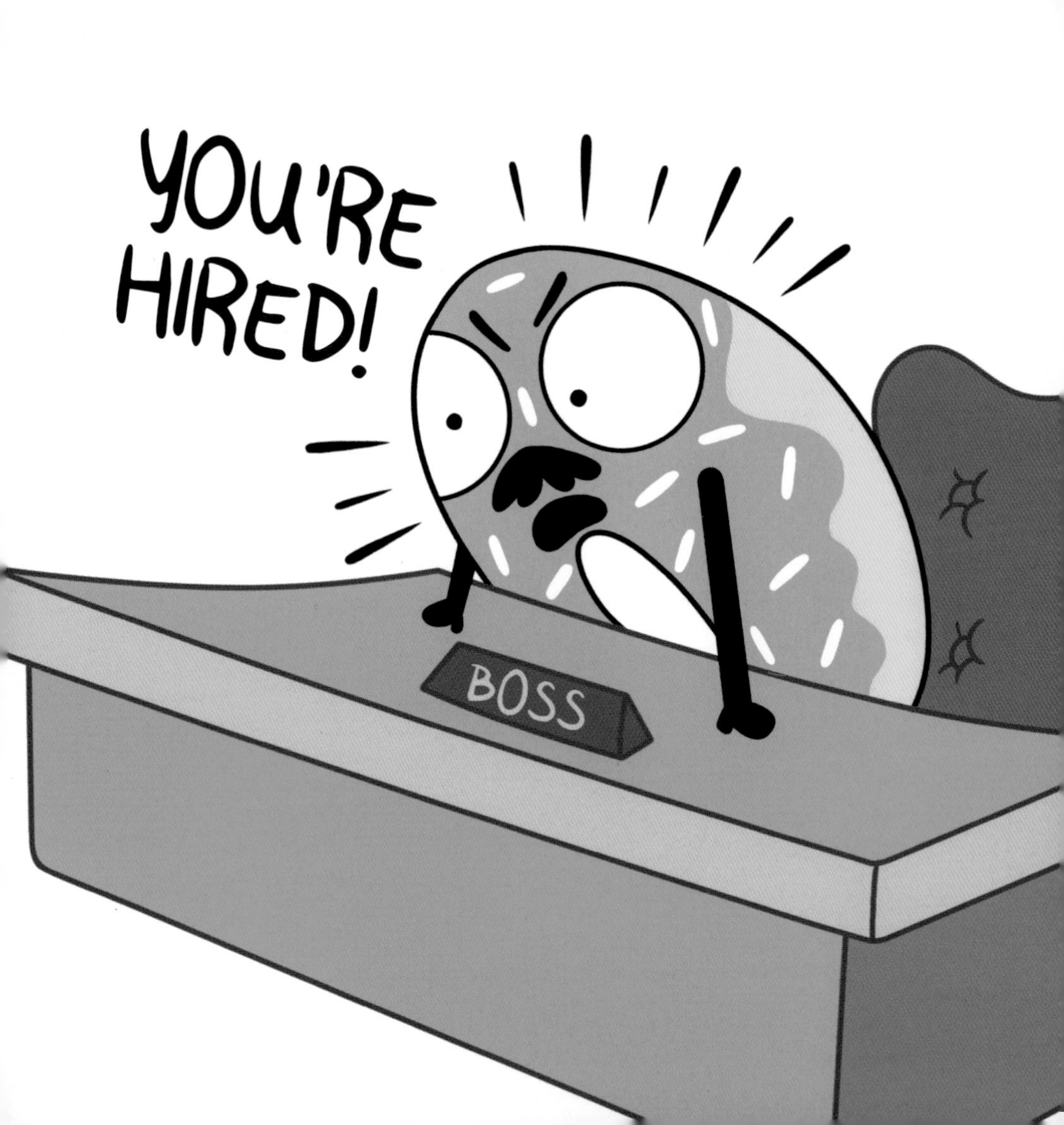
YOU'RE HIRED!
BOSS

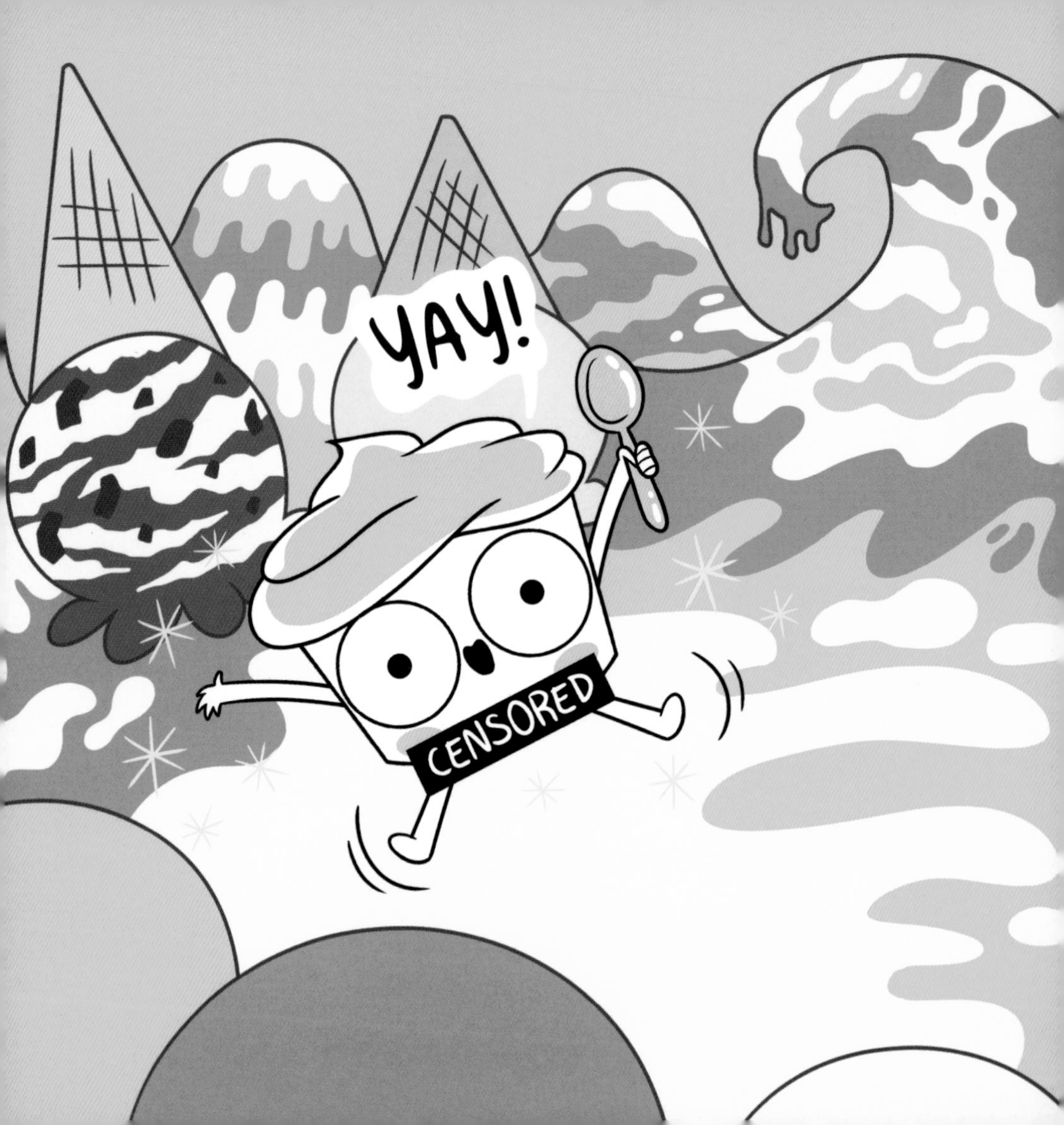
YAY!
CENSORED

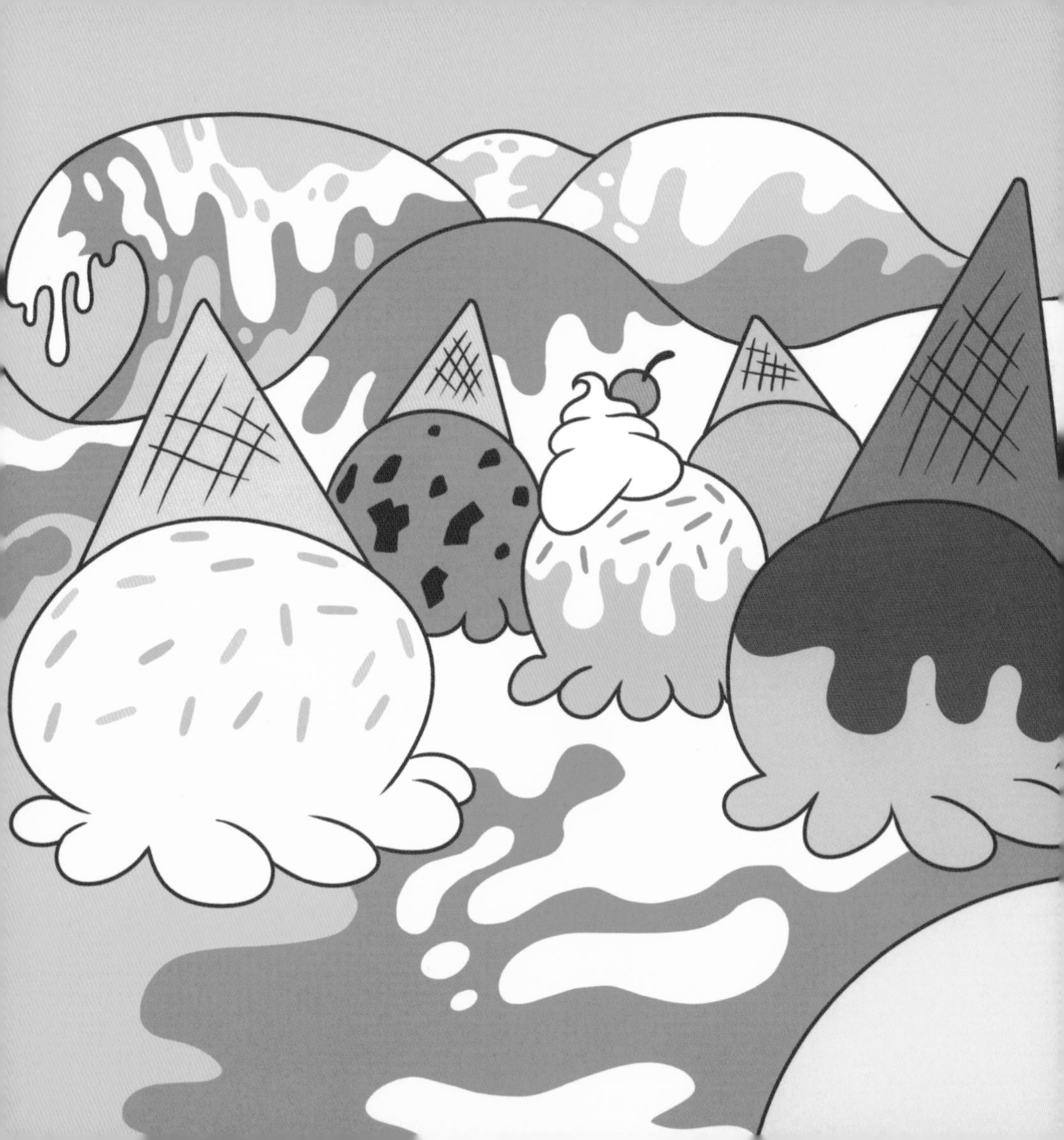

LOVE:
TO DUMP OR
BE DUMPED

LOVE IS A
BEAUTIFUL,

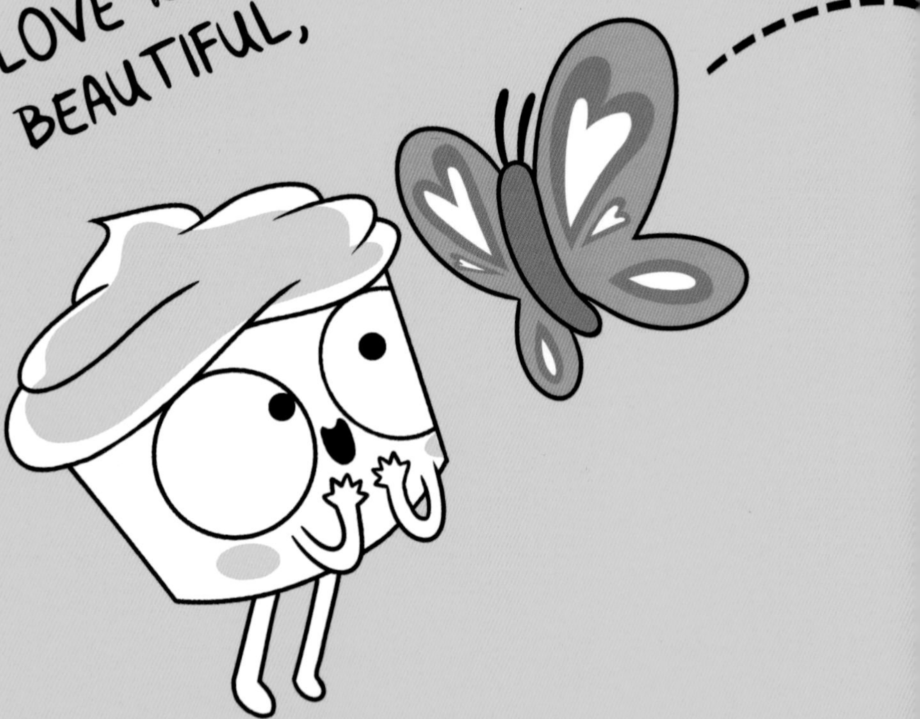

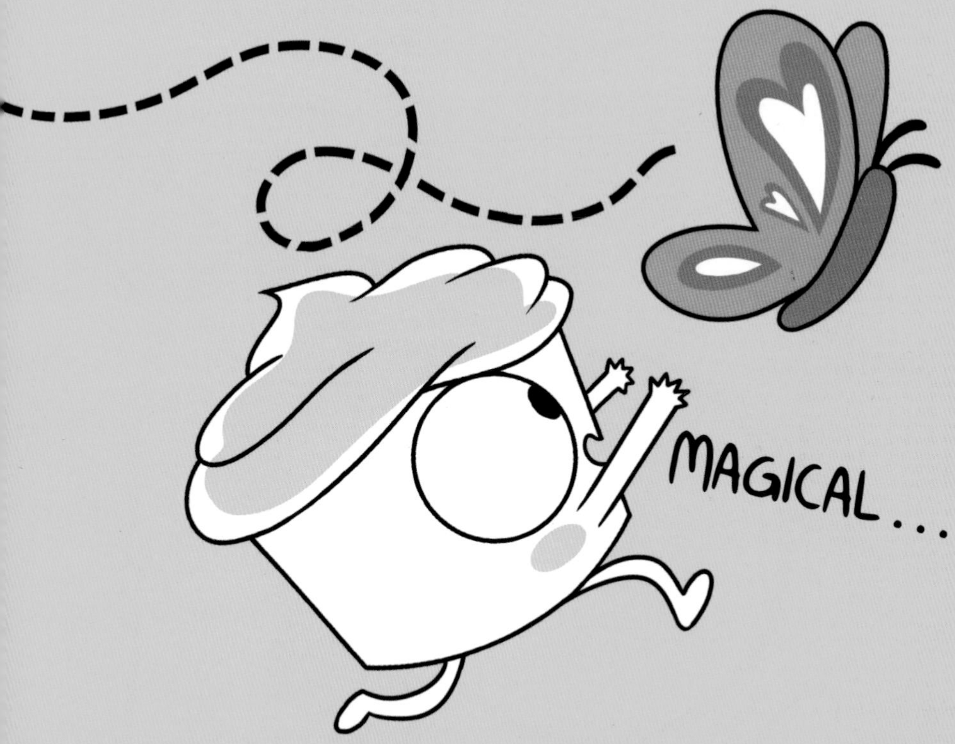
MAGICAL...

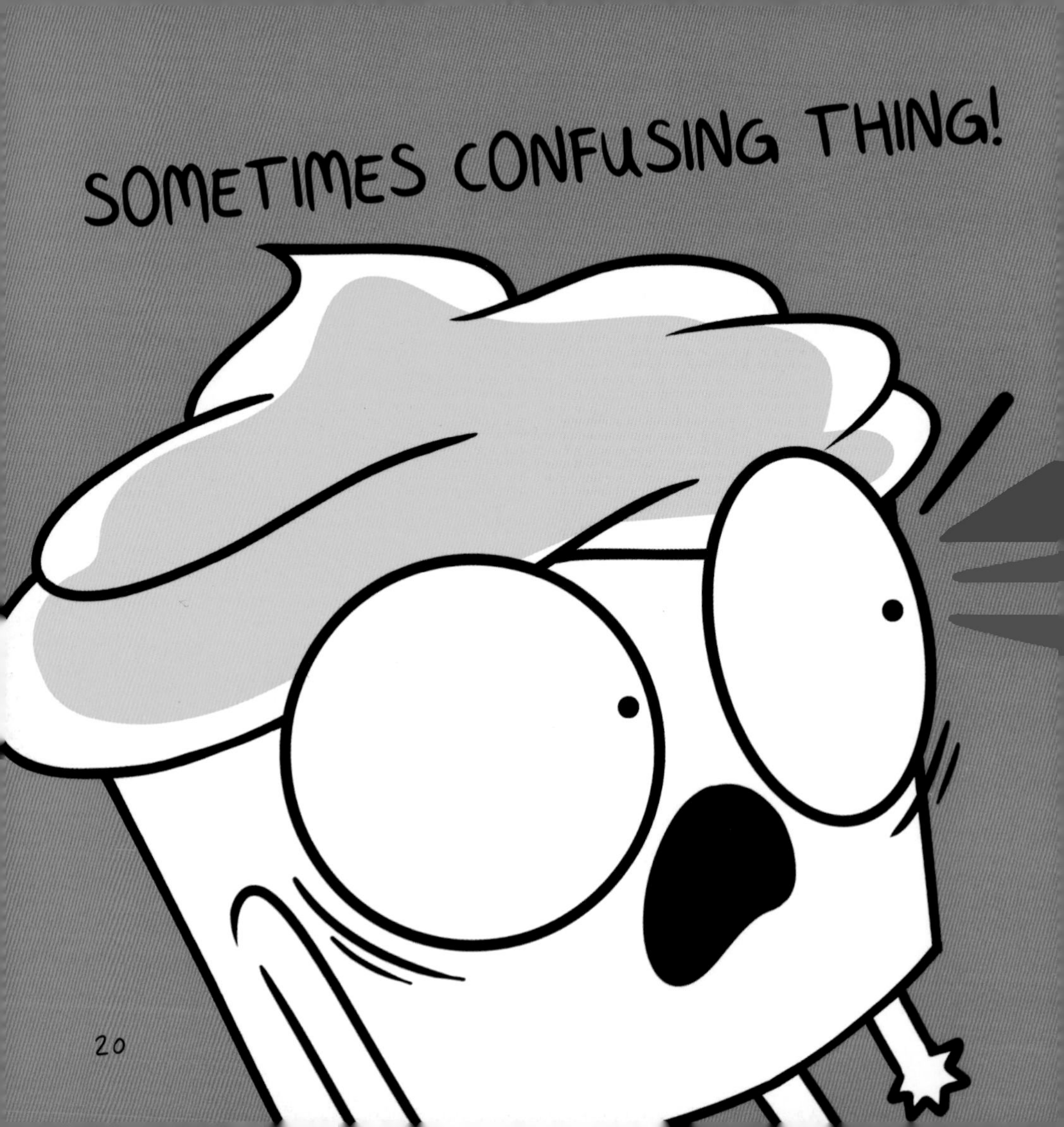
SOMETIMES CONFUSING THING!

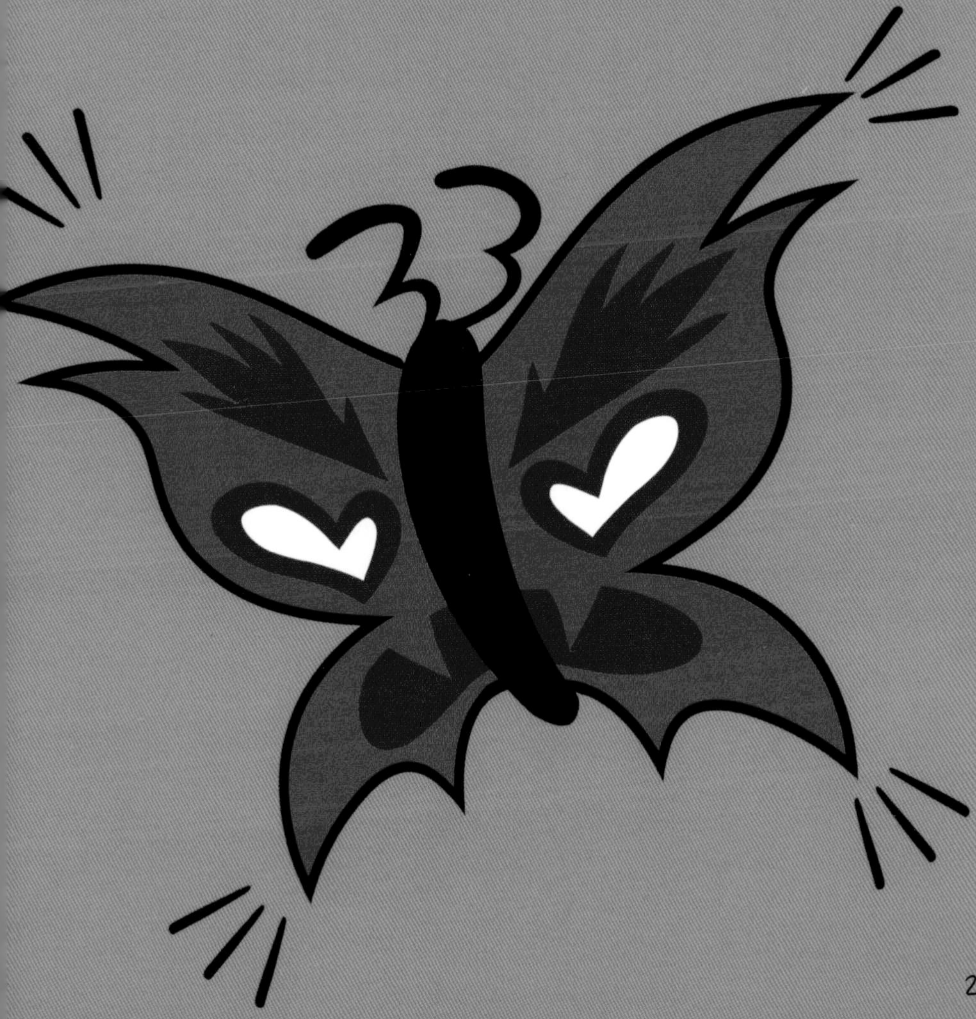

ONE DAY YOU'LL MEET
SOMEONE REALLY SPECIAL.
IT MIGHT FEEL PERFCT...

UNTIL SOMETHING HAPPENS, AND THAT PERSON REVEALS THEMSELF TO BE...

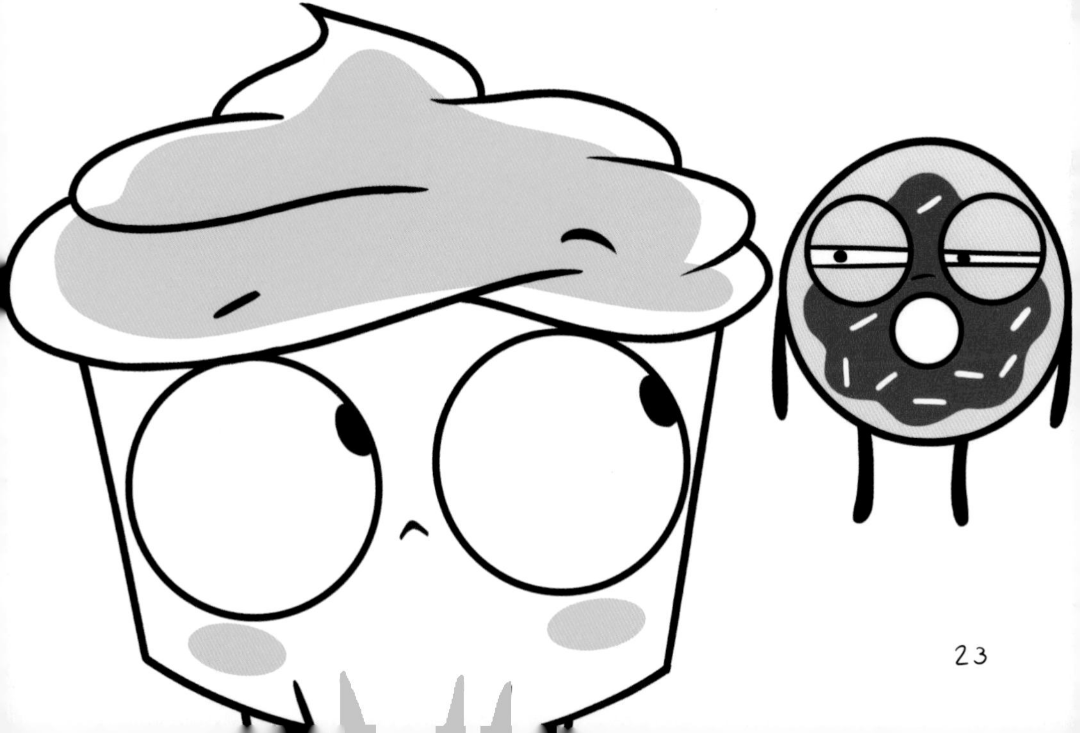

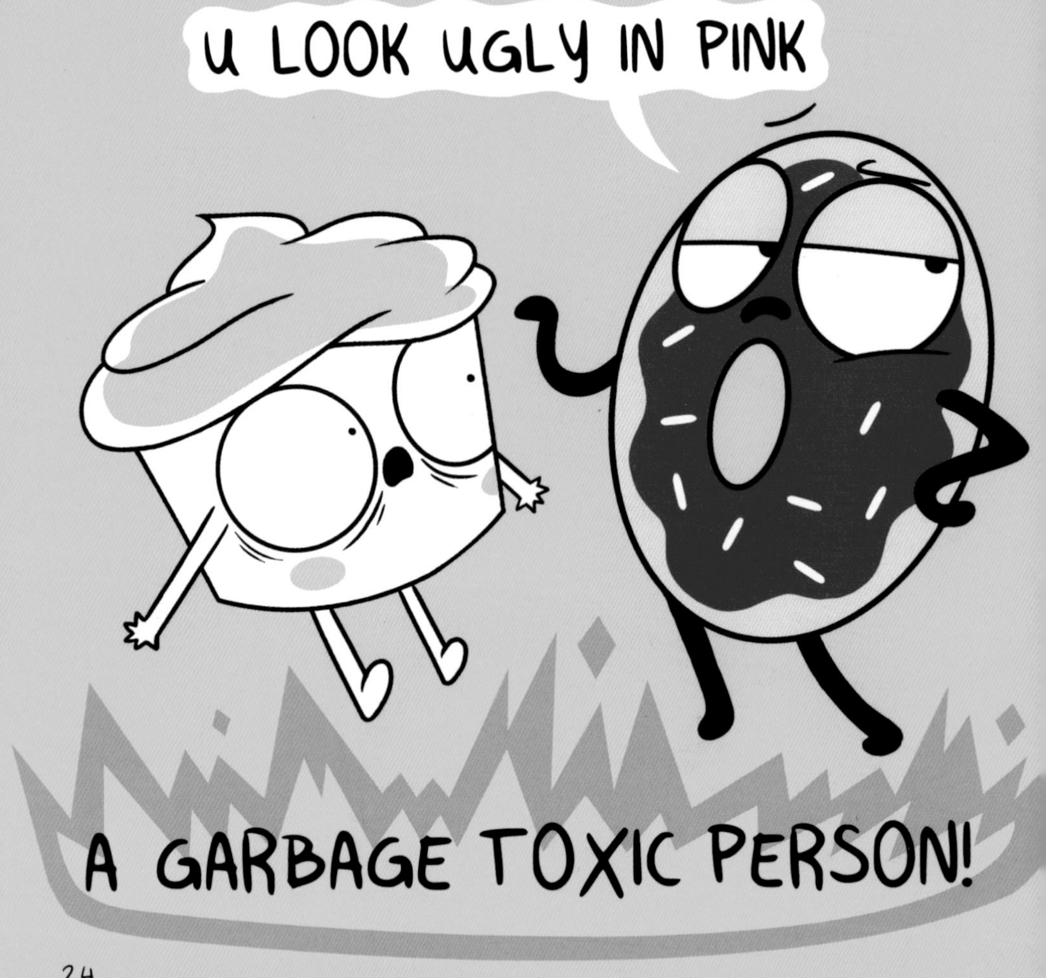
U LOOK UGLY IN PINK
A GARBAGE TOXIC PERSON!

WELL YOU KNOW
WHAT YOU SHOULD DO...

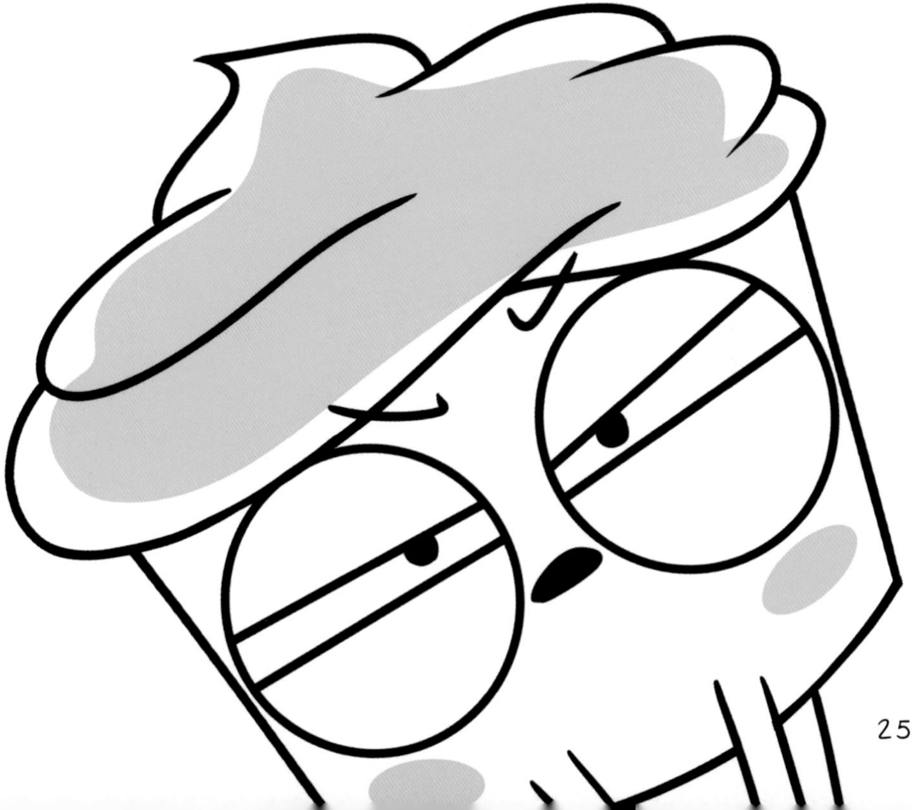

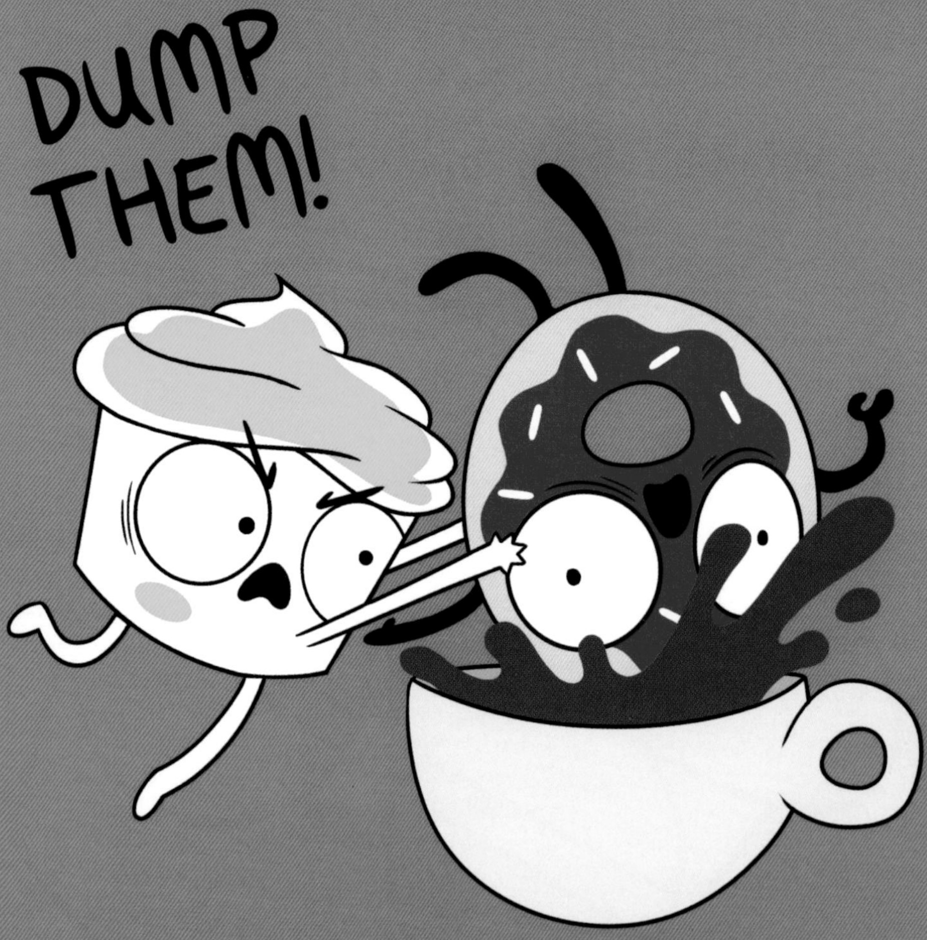
DUMP
THEM!

TO DUMP AND BE DUMPED IS PART OF THE NATURAL COURSE OF FINDING THE RIGHT PARTNER.

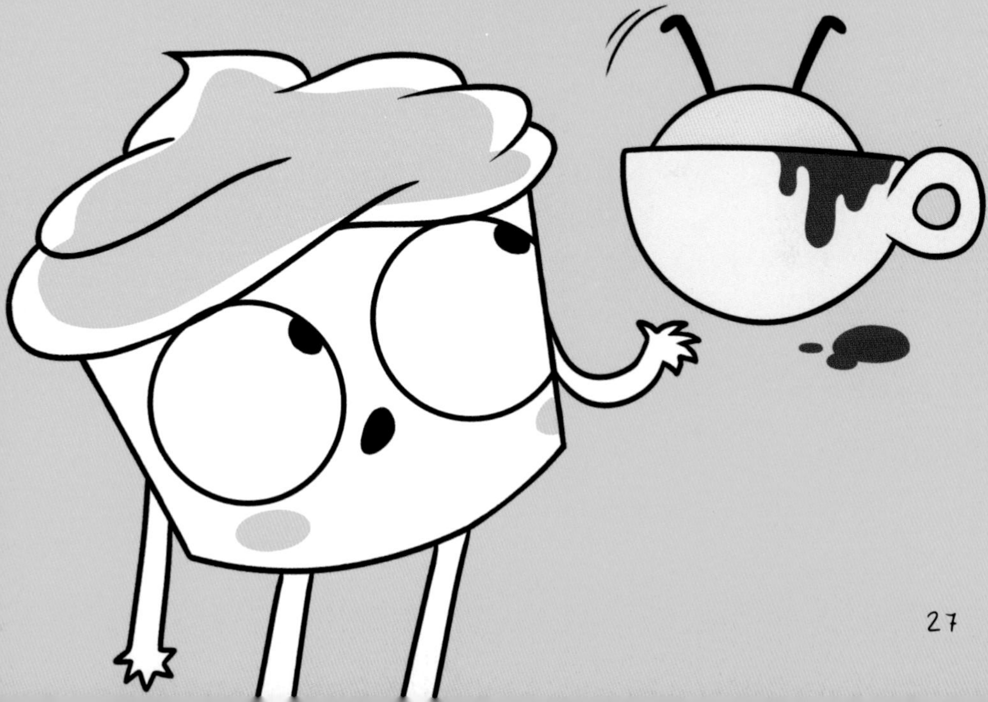

TRY NOT TO LET THE BUMPS IN THE ROAD SLOW YOU DOWN TO FINDING YOUR HAPPY ENDING.

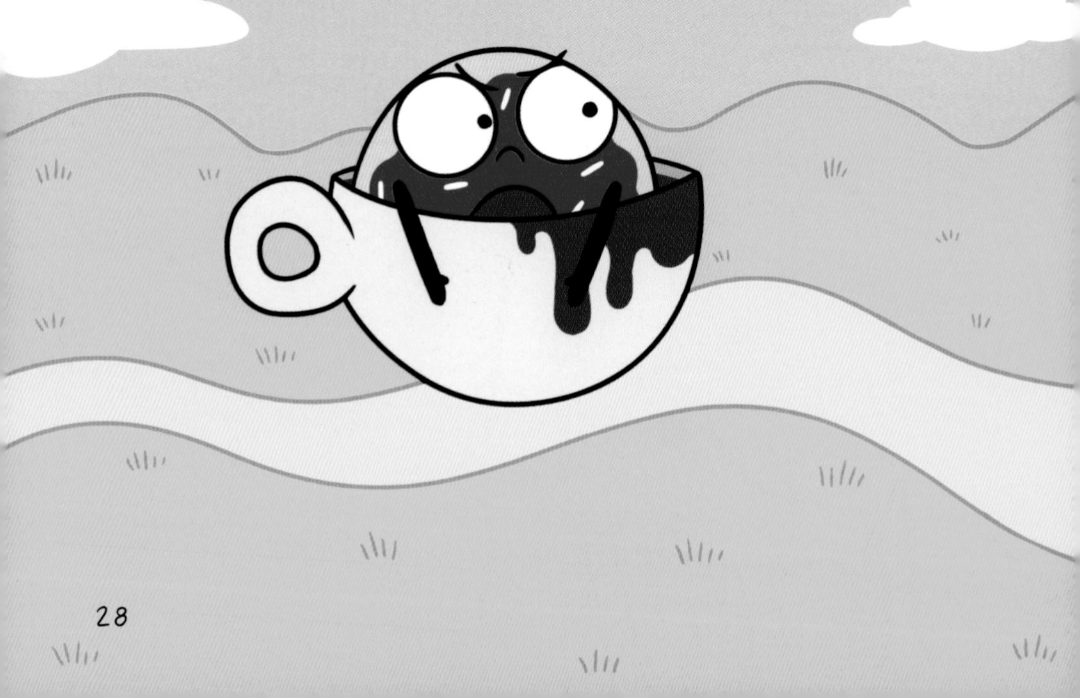

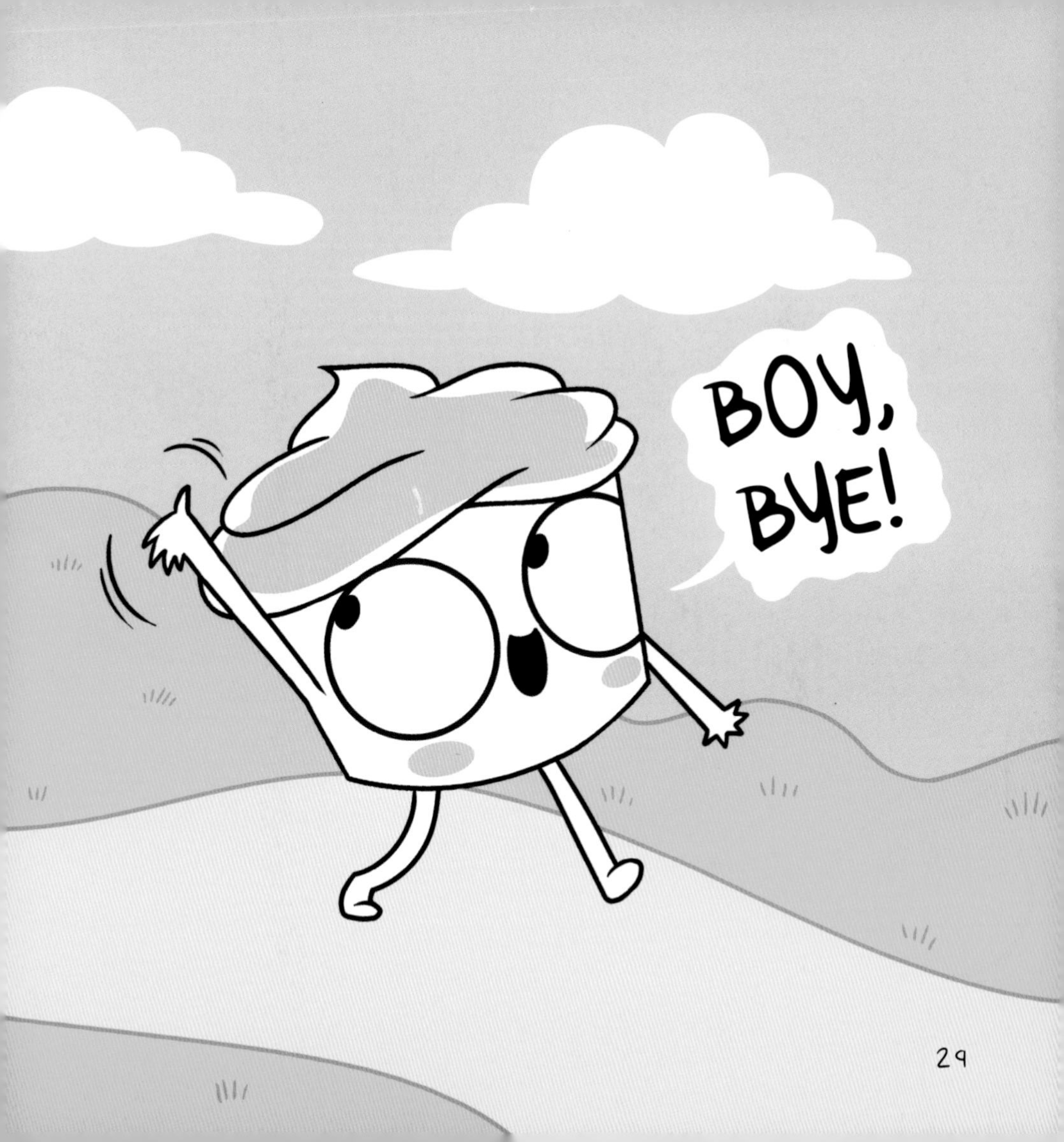
BOY, BYE!

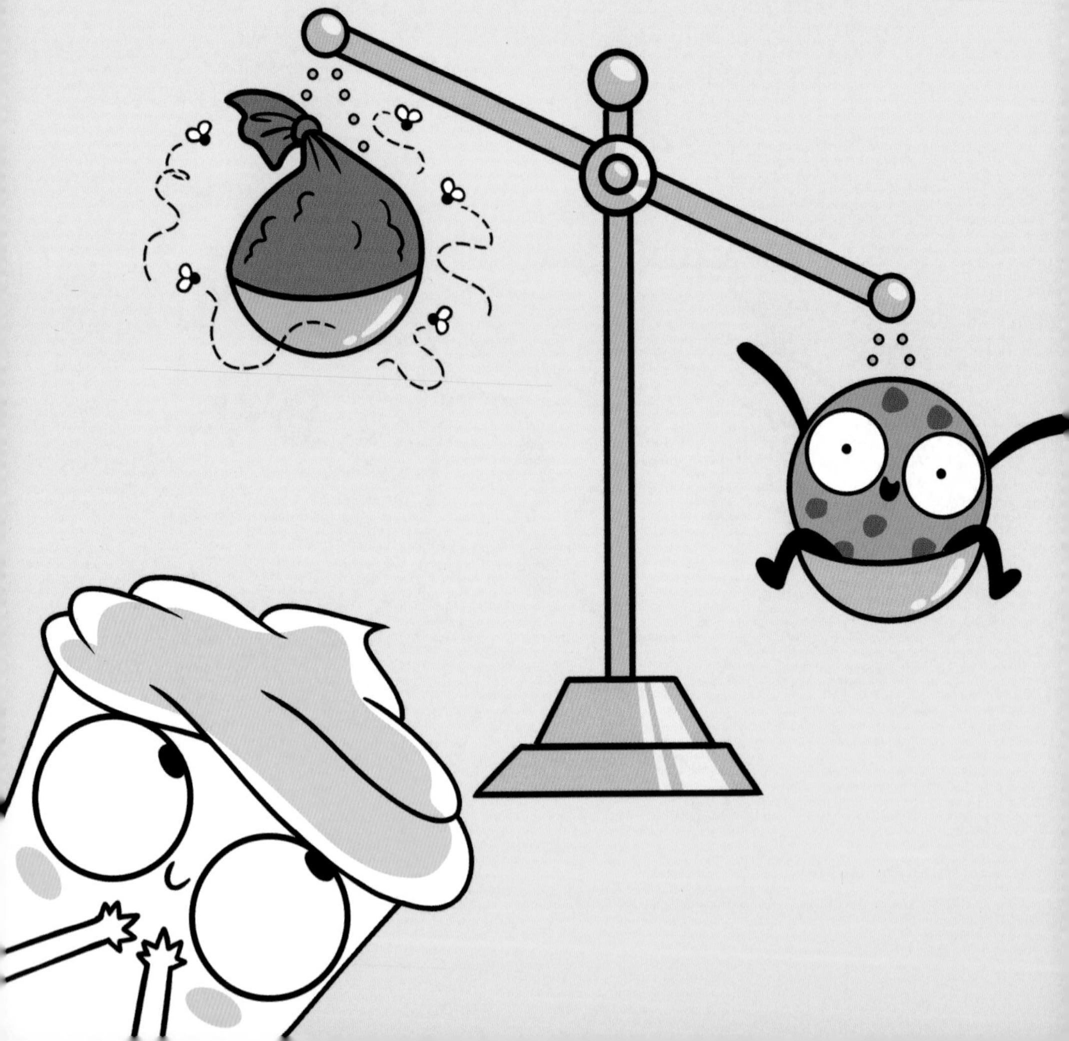

FRIENDSHIP: QUALITY OVER QUANTITY

I'M GONNA MAKE SOME NEW FRIENDS TODAY!

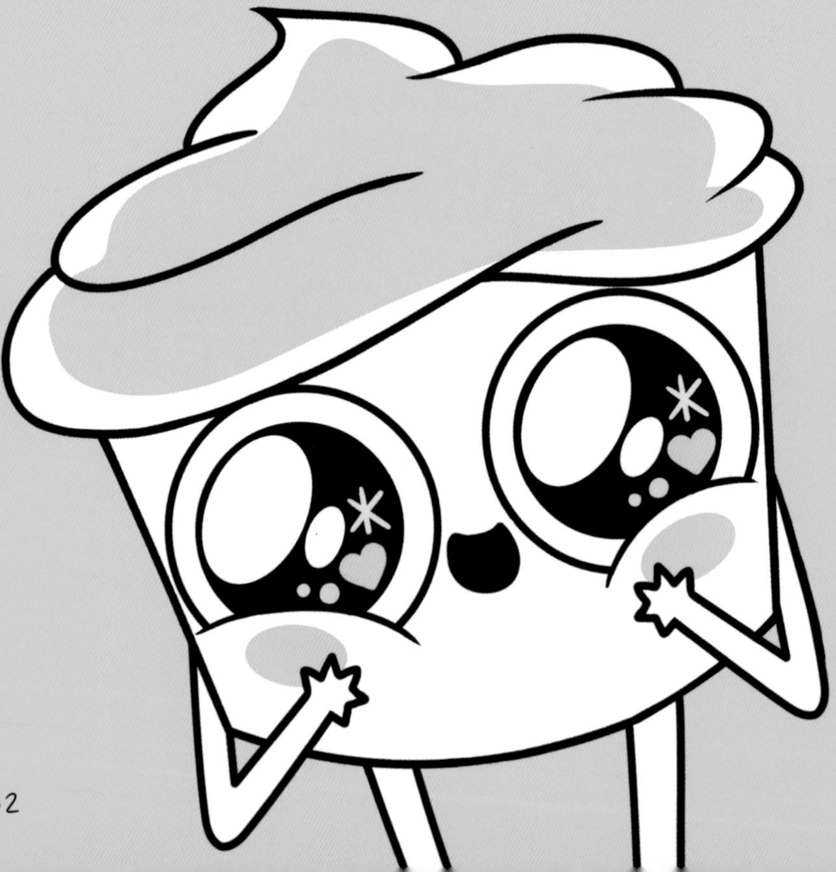

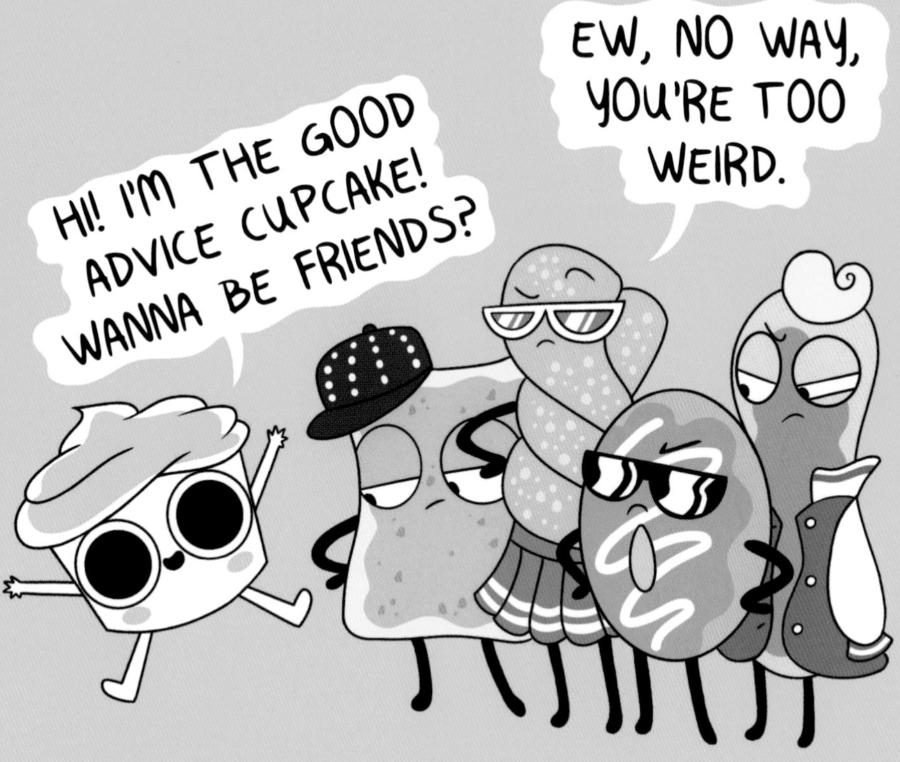
HI! I'M THE GOOD ADVICE CUPCAKE! WANNA BE FRIENDS?
EW, NO WAY, YOU'RE TOO WEIRD.

35

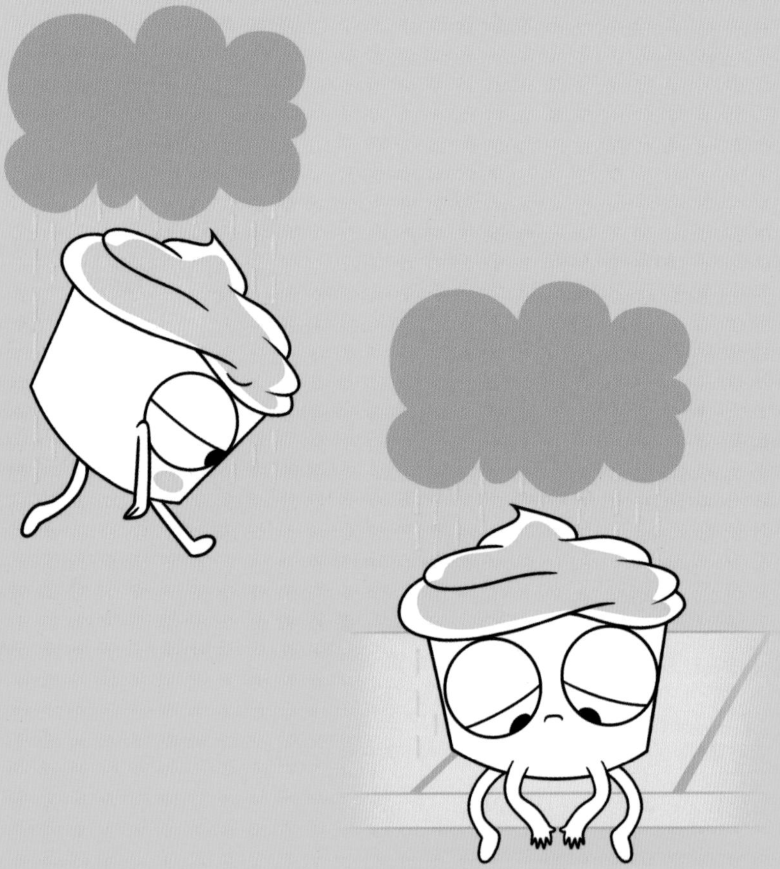

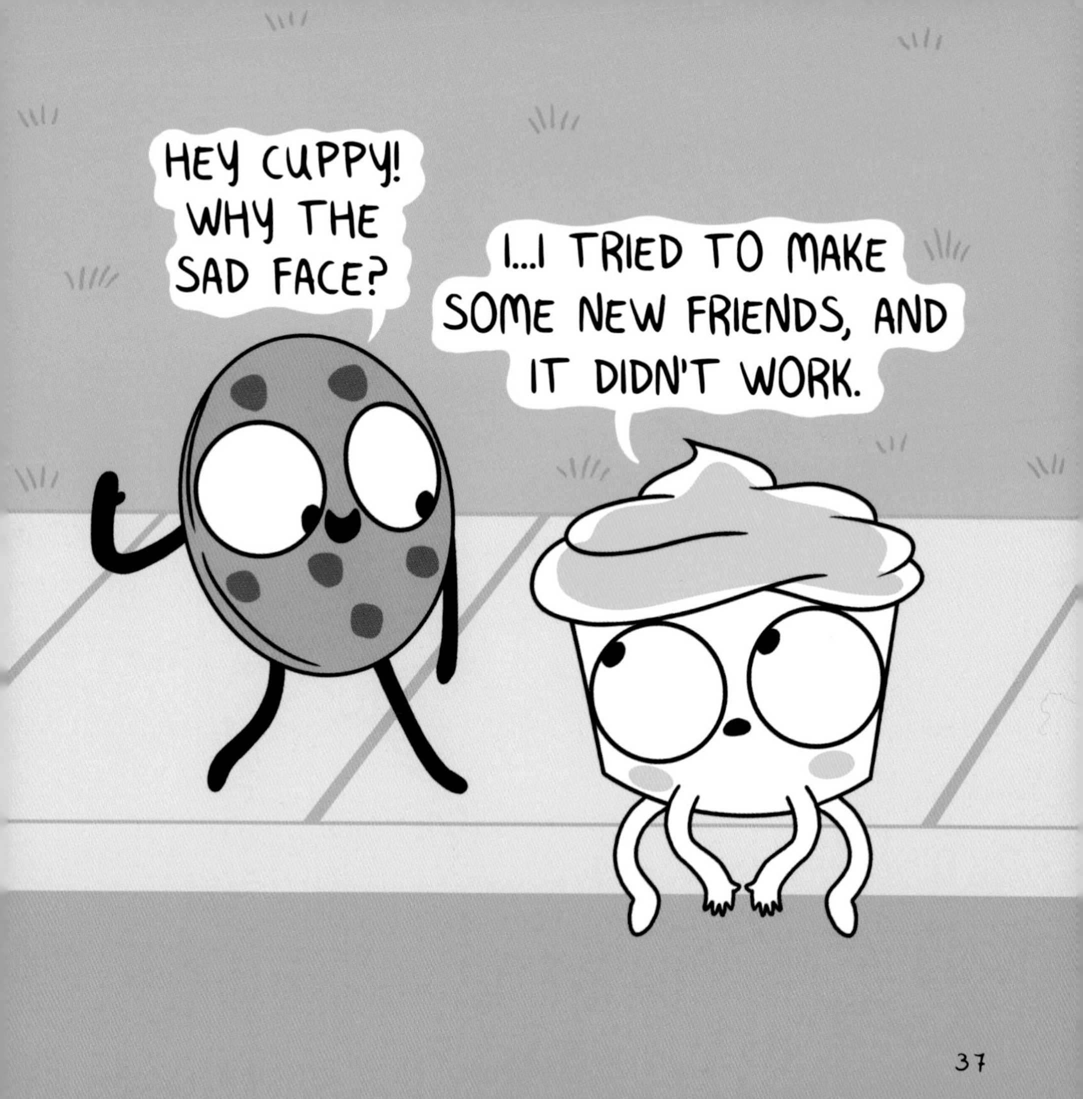
HEY CUPPY! WHY THE SAD FACE?
I...I TRIED TO MAKE SOME NEW FRIENDS, AND IT DIDN'T WORK.

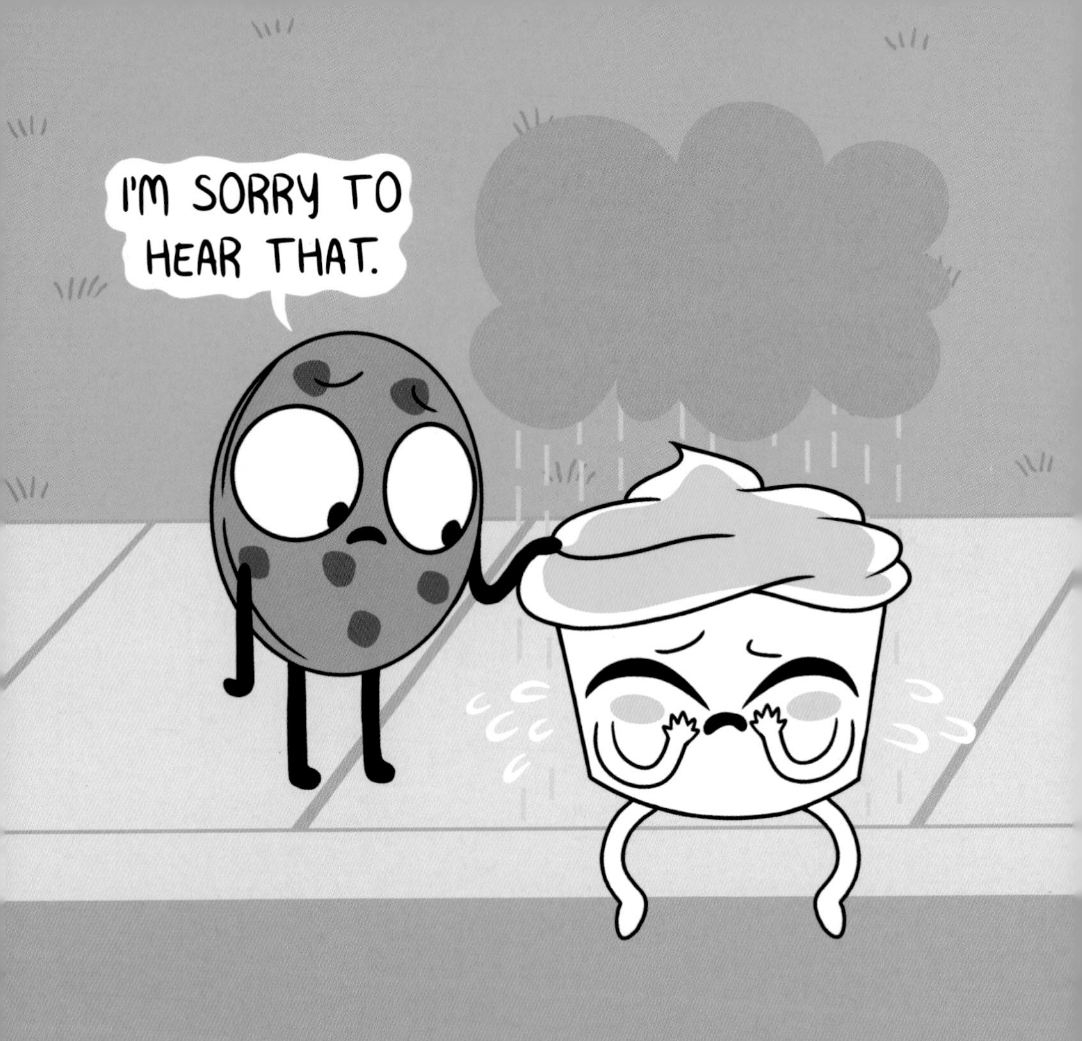
I'M SORRY TO HEAR THAT.

IT'S NOT THE AMOUNT OF FRIENDS YOU HAVE,
IT'S THE QUALITY OF THOSE FRIENDSHIPS.

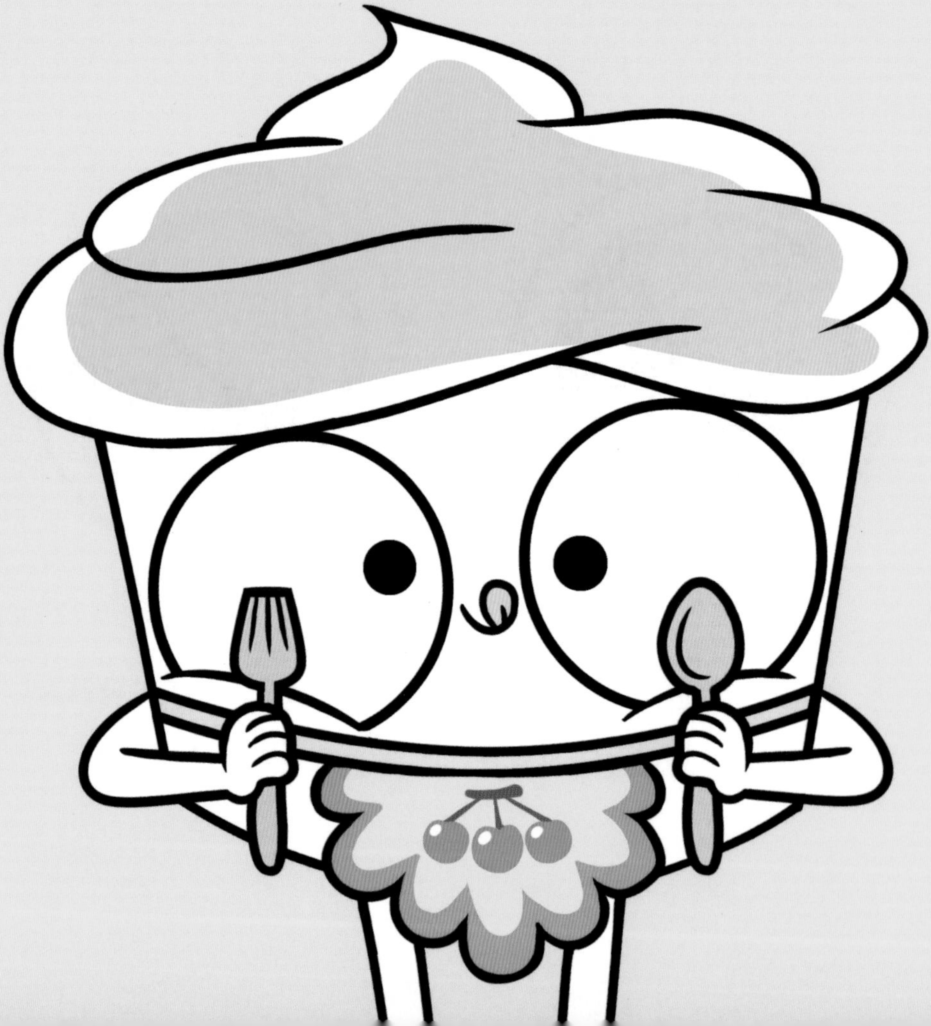

NUTRITION: EATING FOR YOUR BEST SELF

IT IS VERY IMPORTANT TO EAT PROPERLY FOR MAXIMUM ASS KICKING.

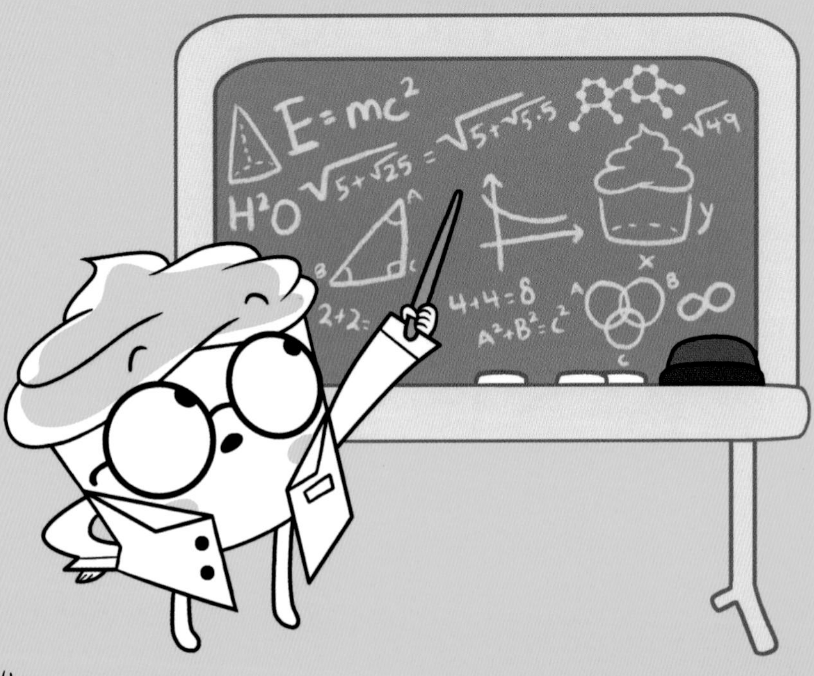

E=mc²
H²O
√5+√25 = √5+√5.5
√49
4+4=8
A²+B²=C²
2+2=

THIS IS WHY I RECOMMEND A DIET FULL OF A WIDE VARIETY OF HEALTHY OPTIONS.

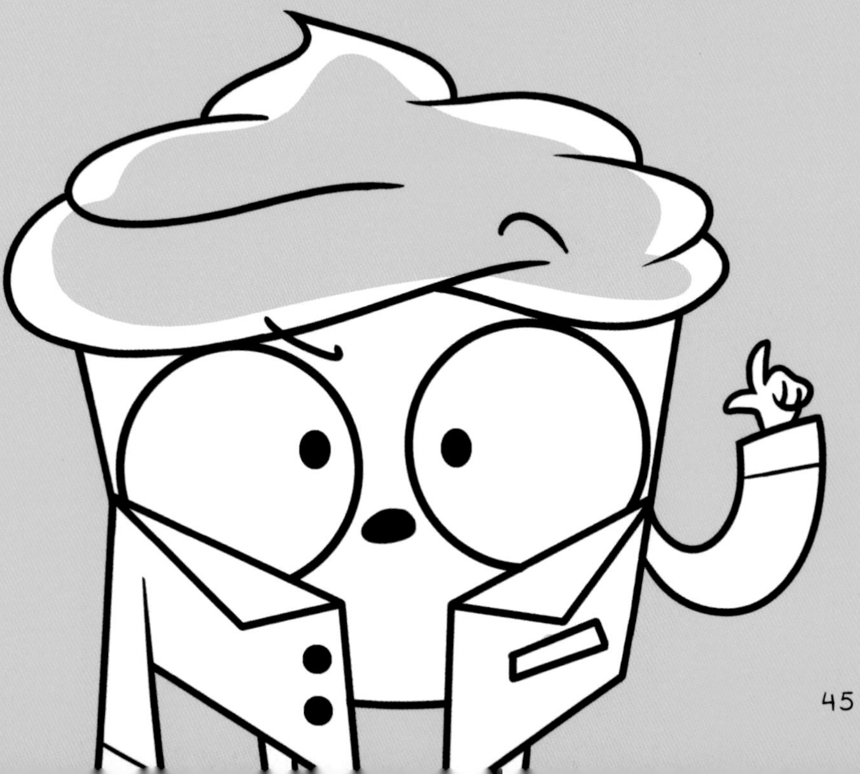

LET'S HEAD ON DOWN TO THE SUPERMARKET TO SEE AN EXAMPLE OF PERFECT FOODS TO BUY FOR LIVING YOUR BEST LIFE...

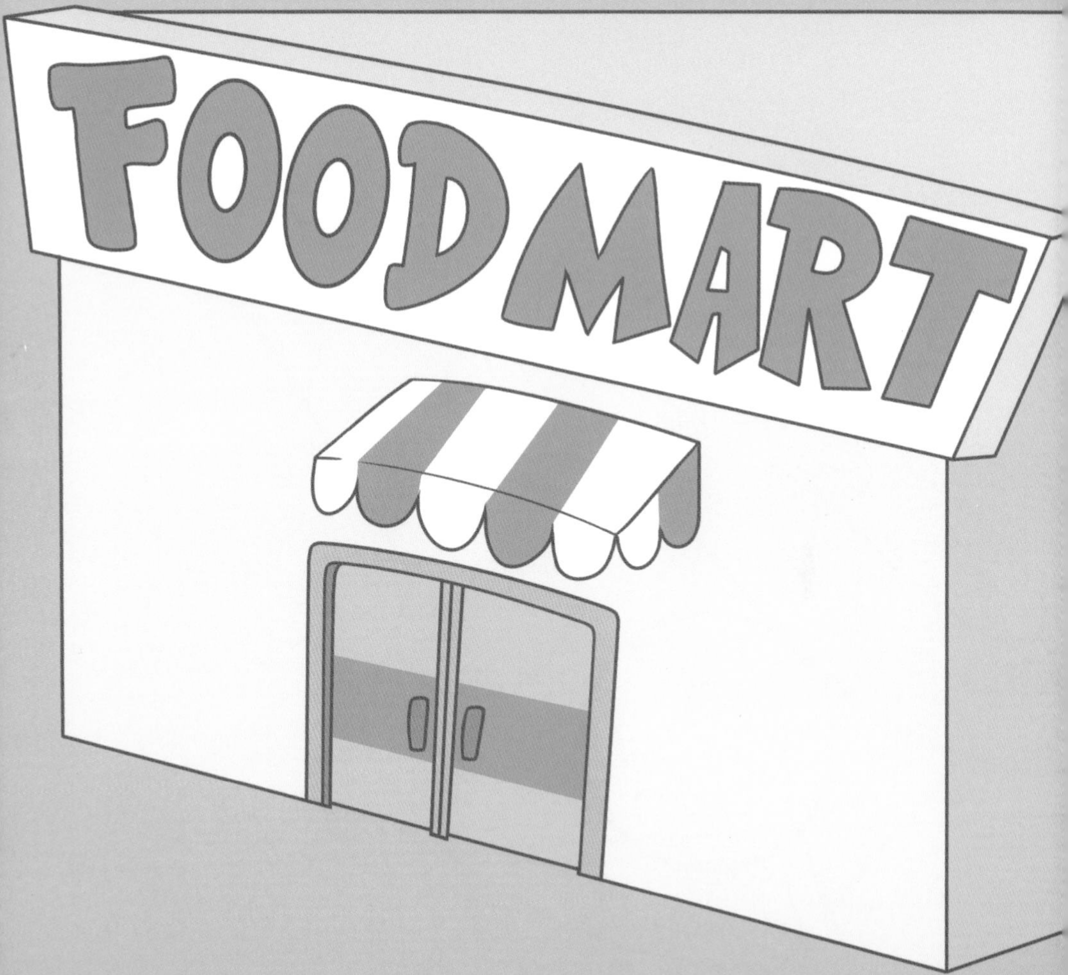
FOOD MART

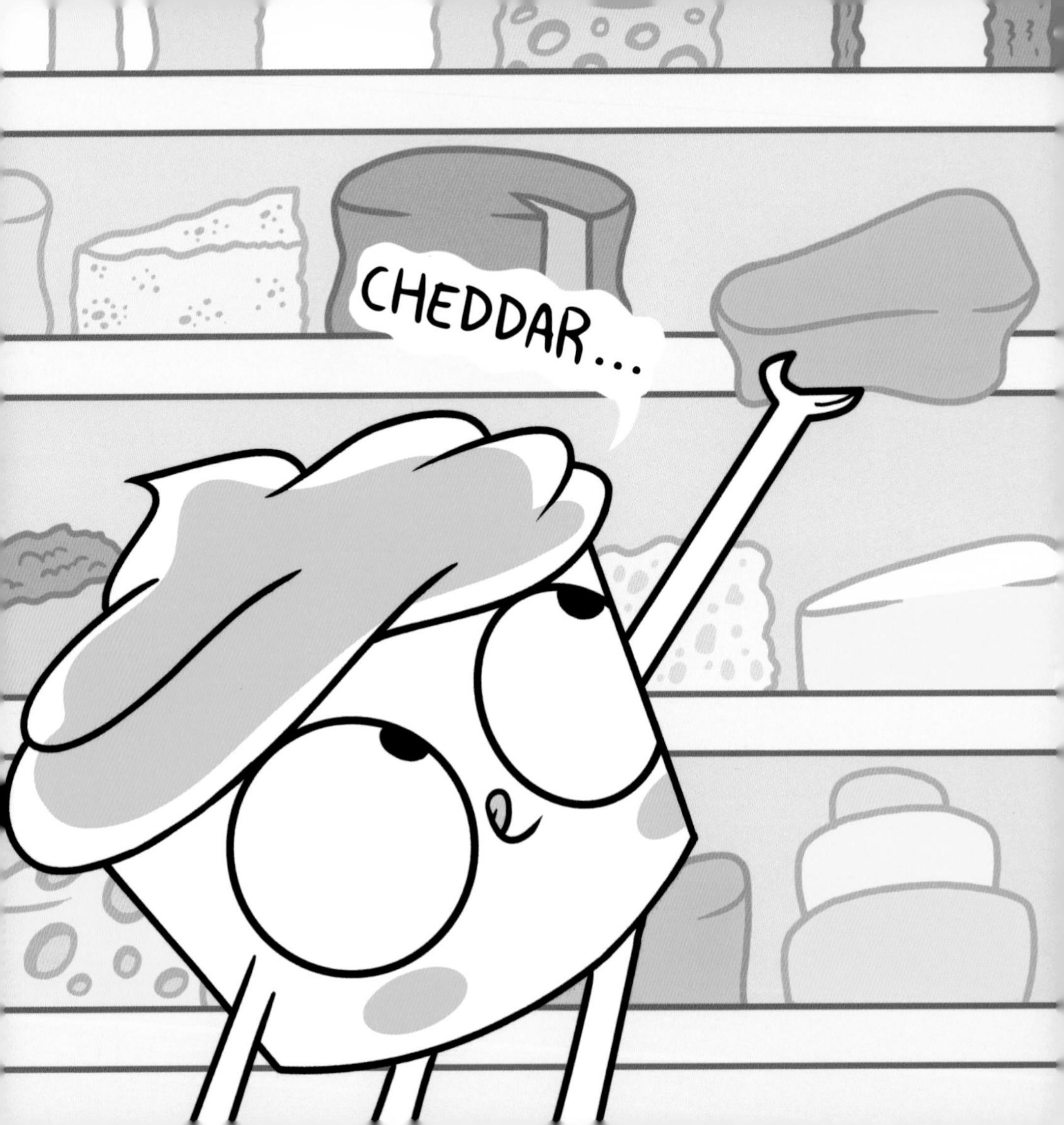
CHEDDAR...

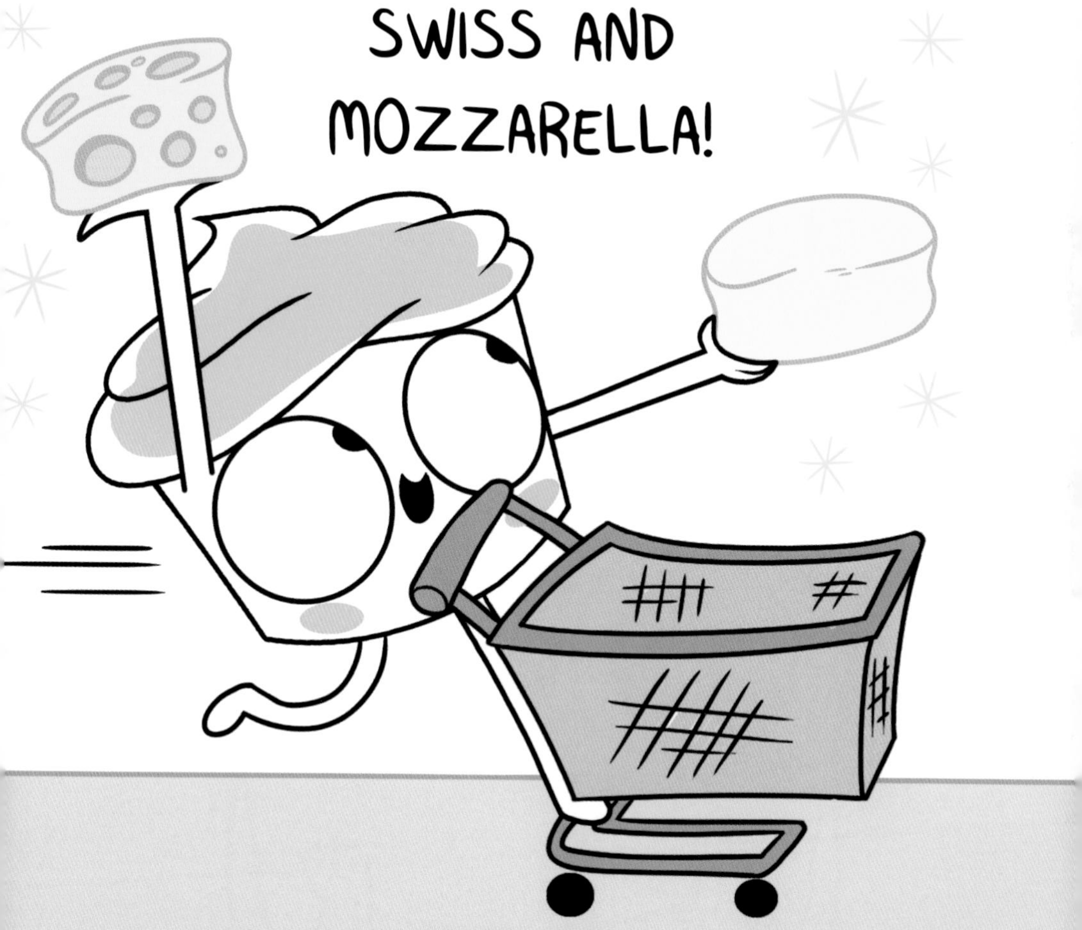
SWISS AND
MOZZARELLA!

MUENSTER AND BRIE!

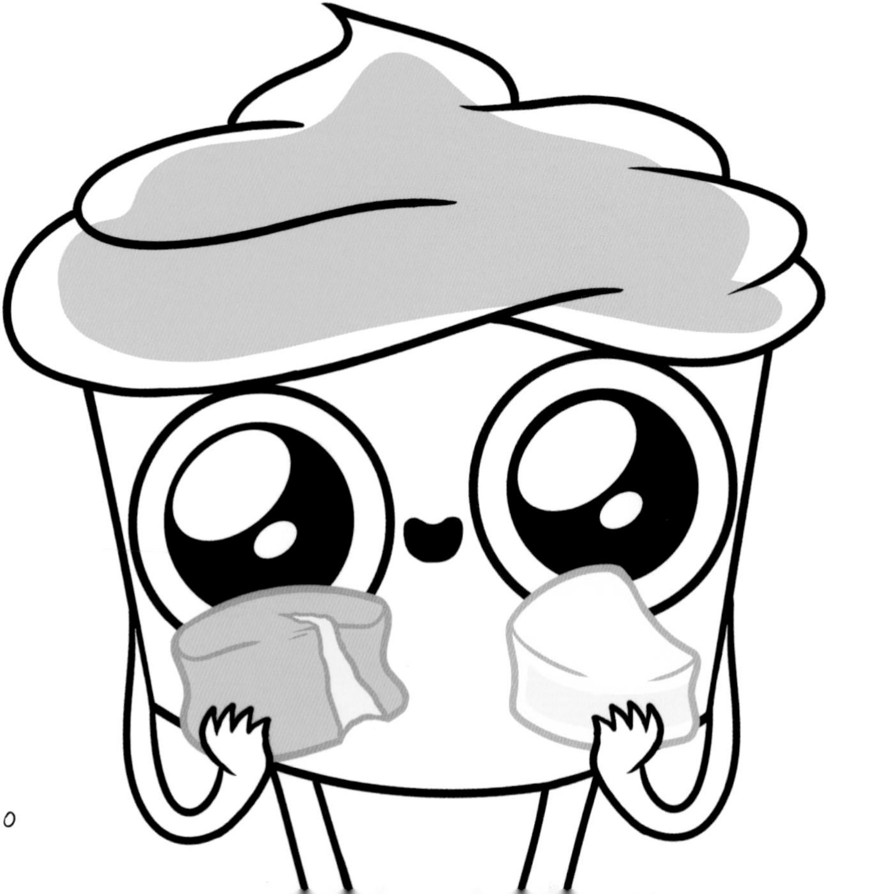

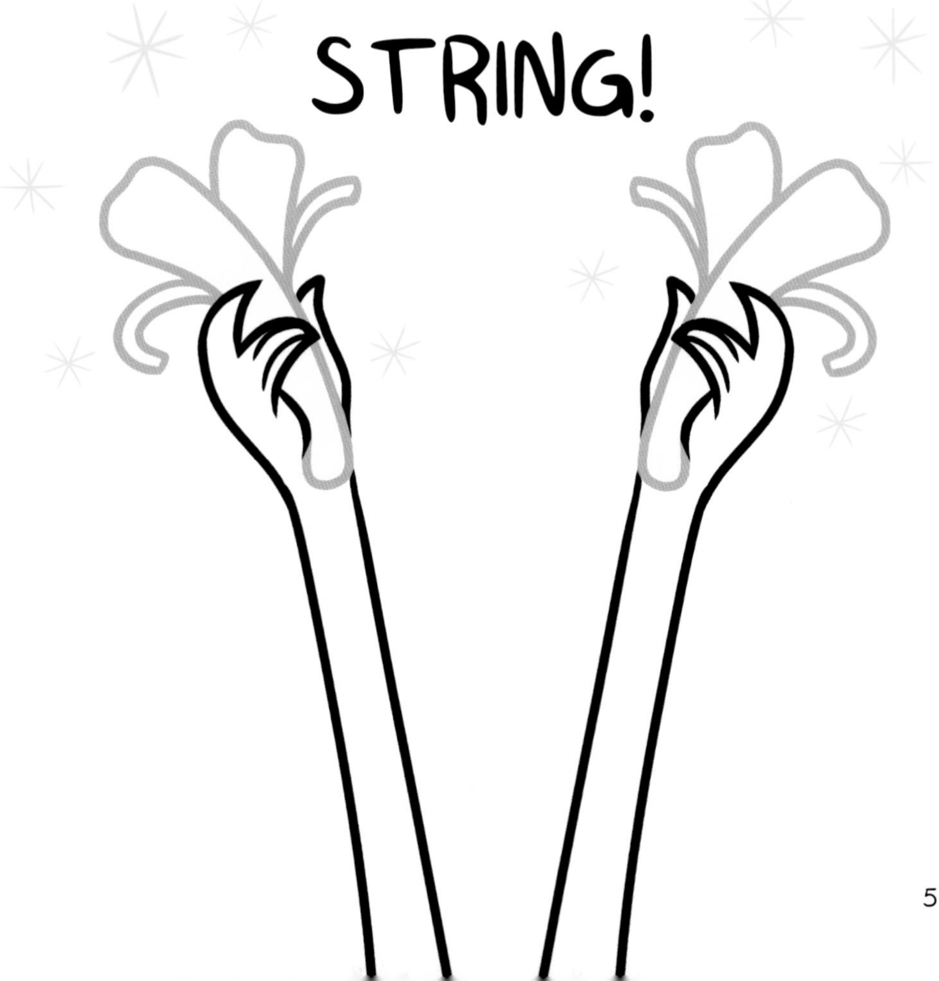
STRING!

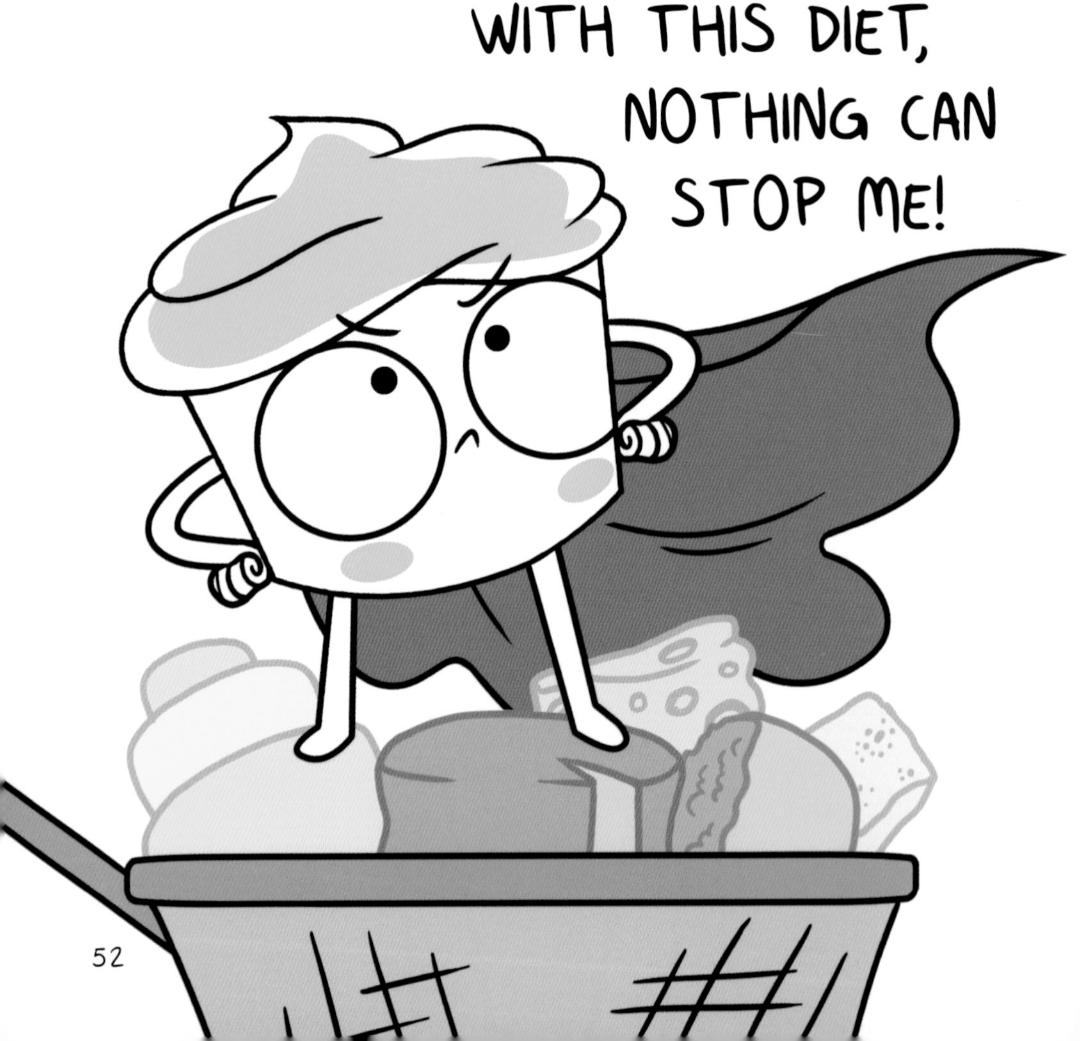
WITH THIS DIET,
NOTHING CAN
STOP ME!

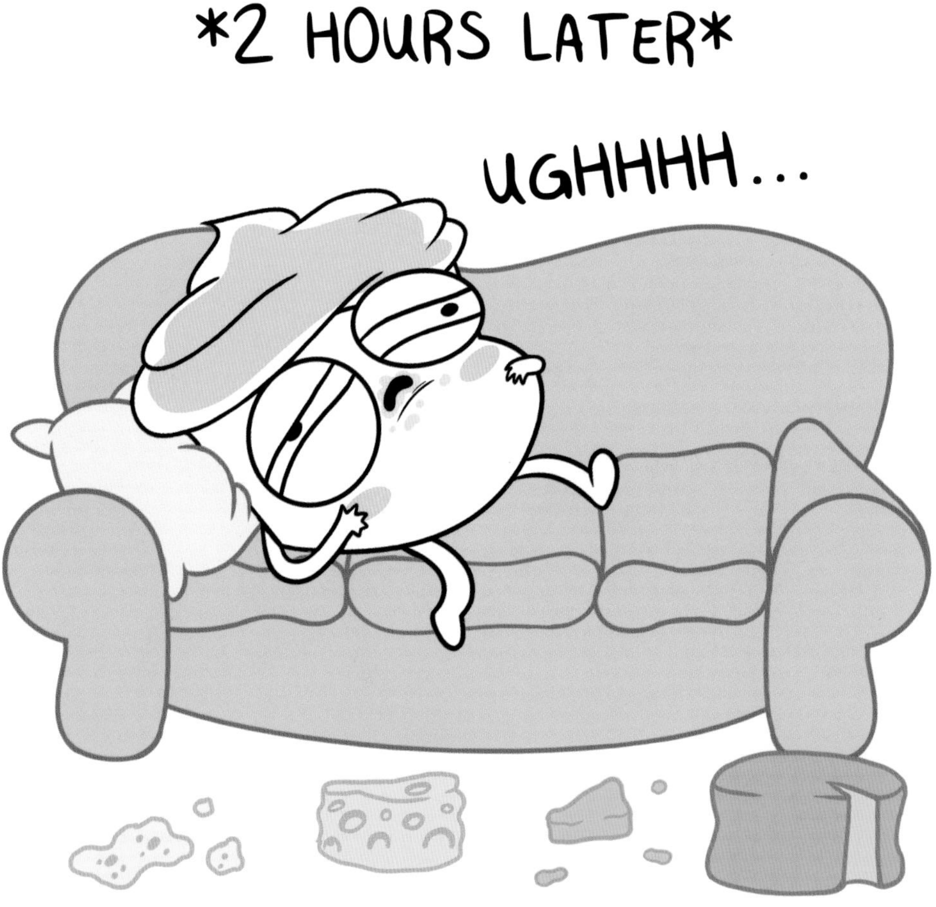
2 HOURS LATER
UGHHHH...

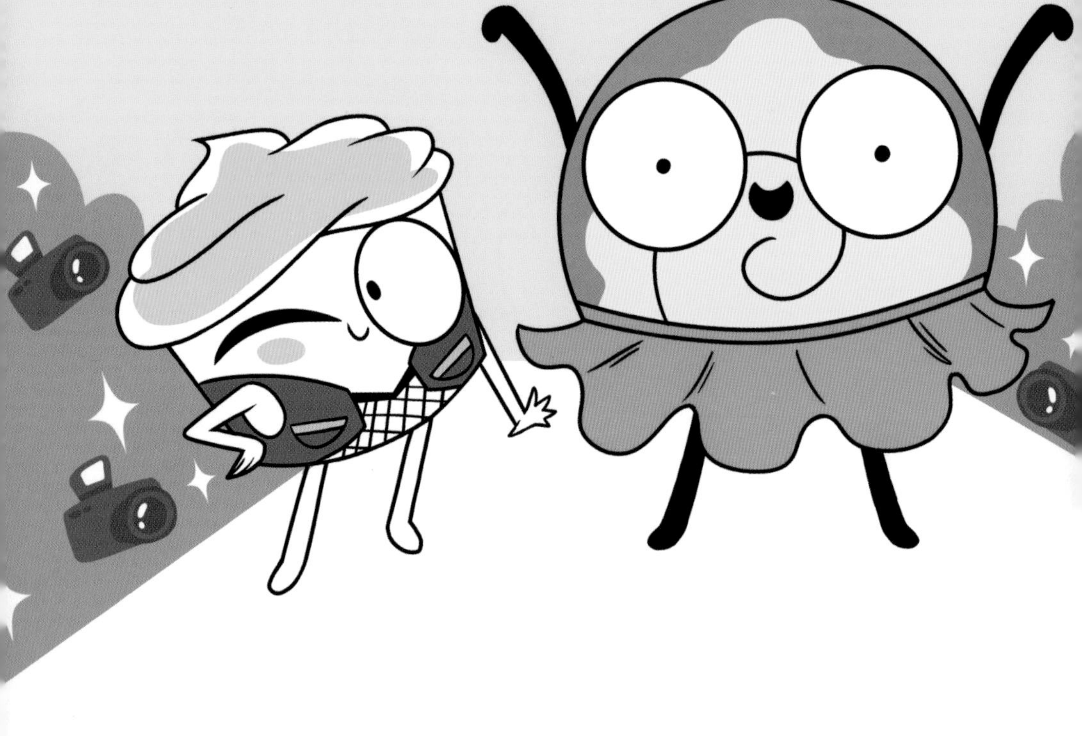

FASHION: CLOTHES TO COMPLEMENT YOUR SHAPE

AS YOU CAN SEE, BUN AND I
HAVE THE IDEAL BODY SHAPES:
ROUND ON TOP, WIDE IN THE MIDDLE,
AND FLAT ON THE BOTTOM OR...

COMPLETELY ROUND!

EVEN IF YOU DON'T HAVE A PERFECT PHYSIQUE LIKE US, IT DOESN'T MEAN YOU CAN'T LOOK AMAZING BY DRESSING FOR YOUR SHAPE!

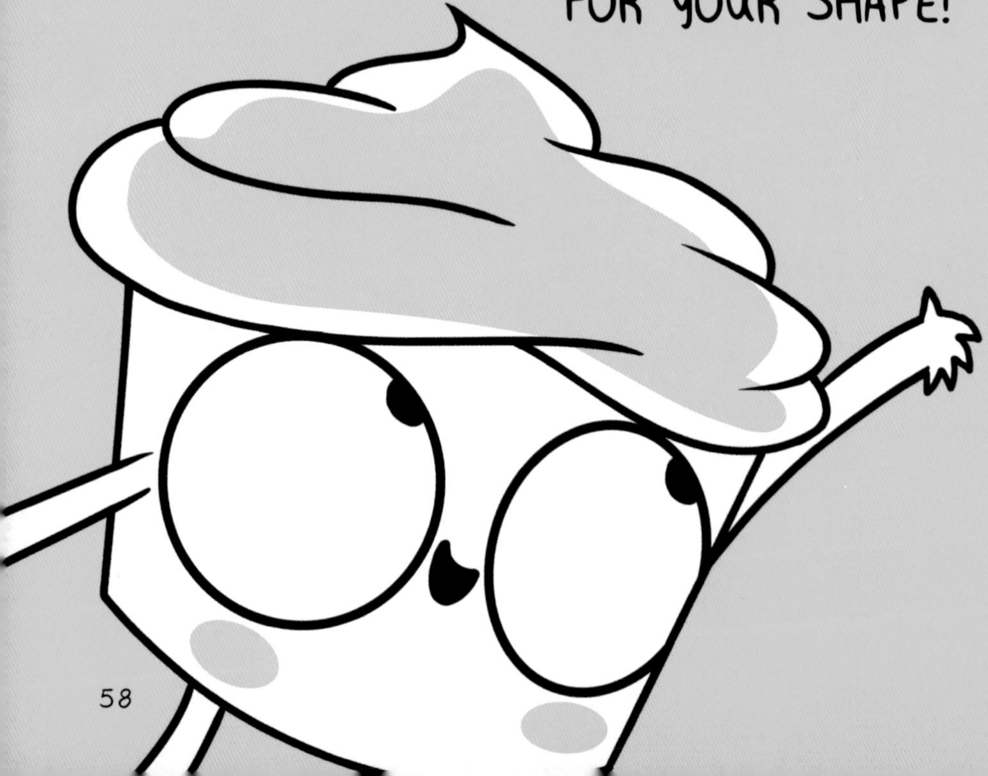

FIND YOUR SHAPE AND NUMBER AND GO TO THE ANSWER KEY TO FIND OUT WHAT YOU SHOULD BE WEARING!

1.

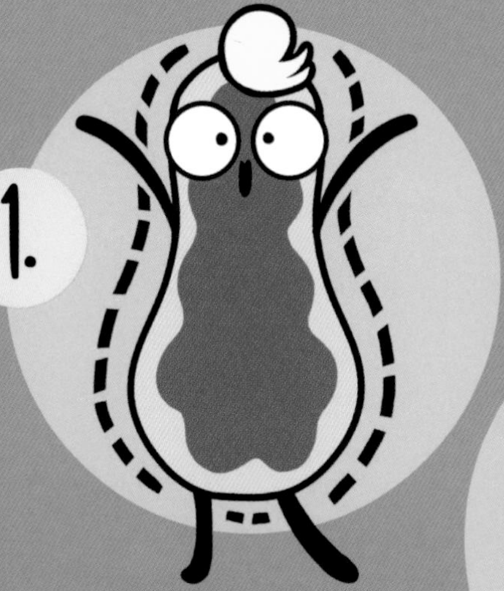

ÉCLAIR SHAPE

2.

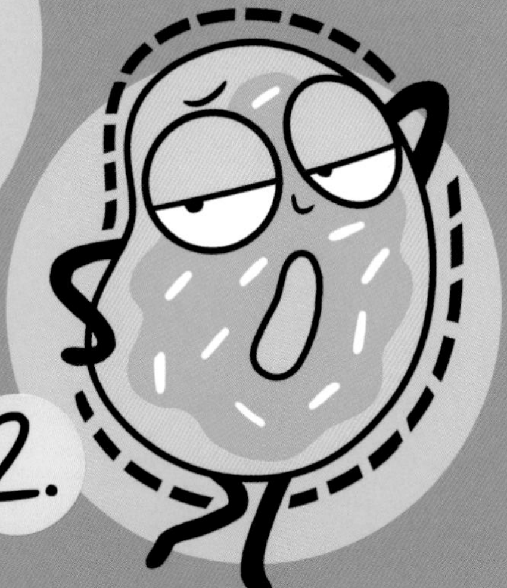

DONUT SHAPE

3.

CROISSANT SHAPE

4.

CAKE SHAPE

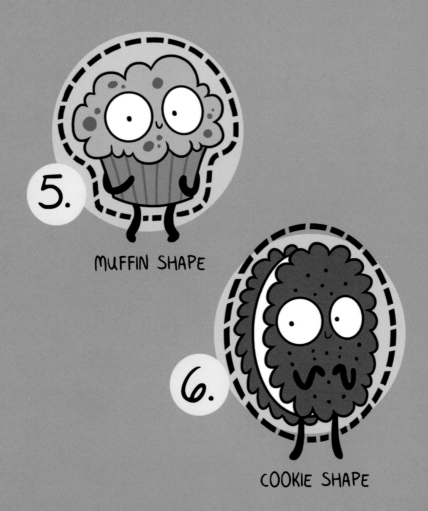

5. MUFFIN SHAPE

6. COOKIE SHAPE

61

ANSWER-KEY SHAPES 1-6:

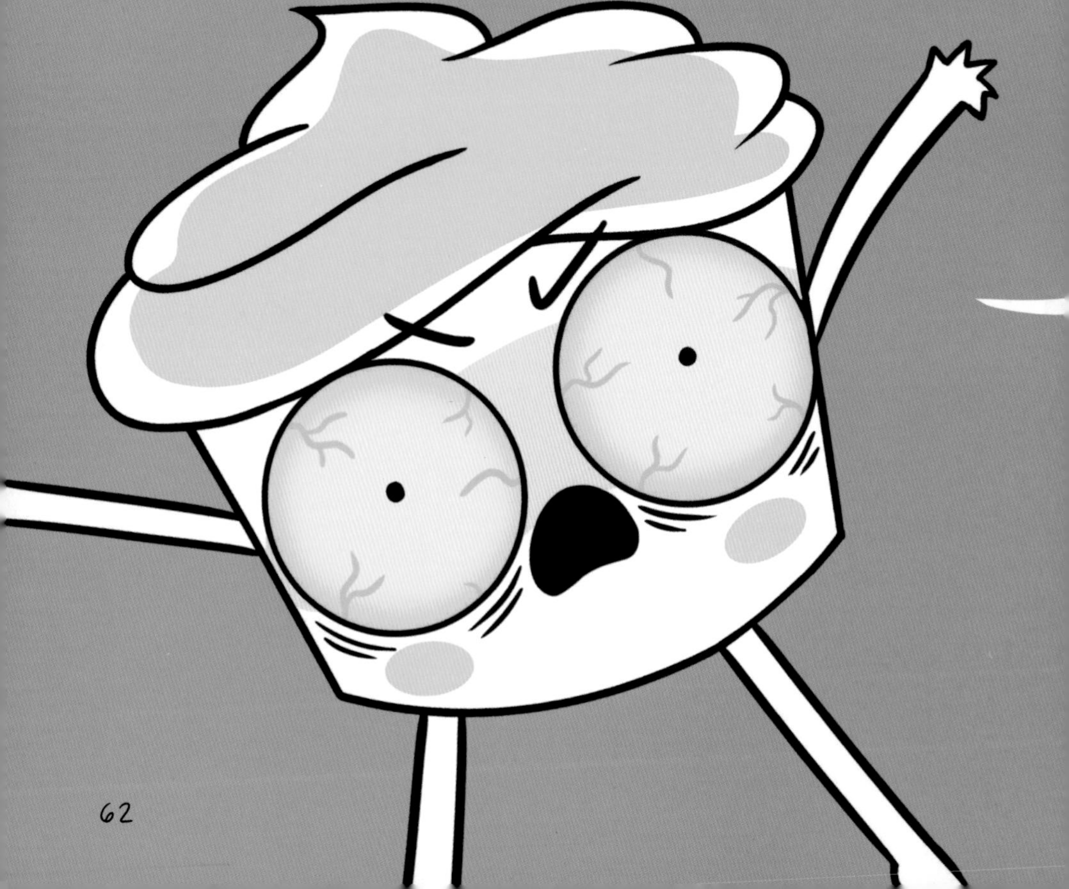

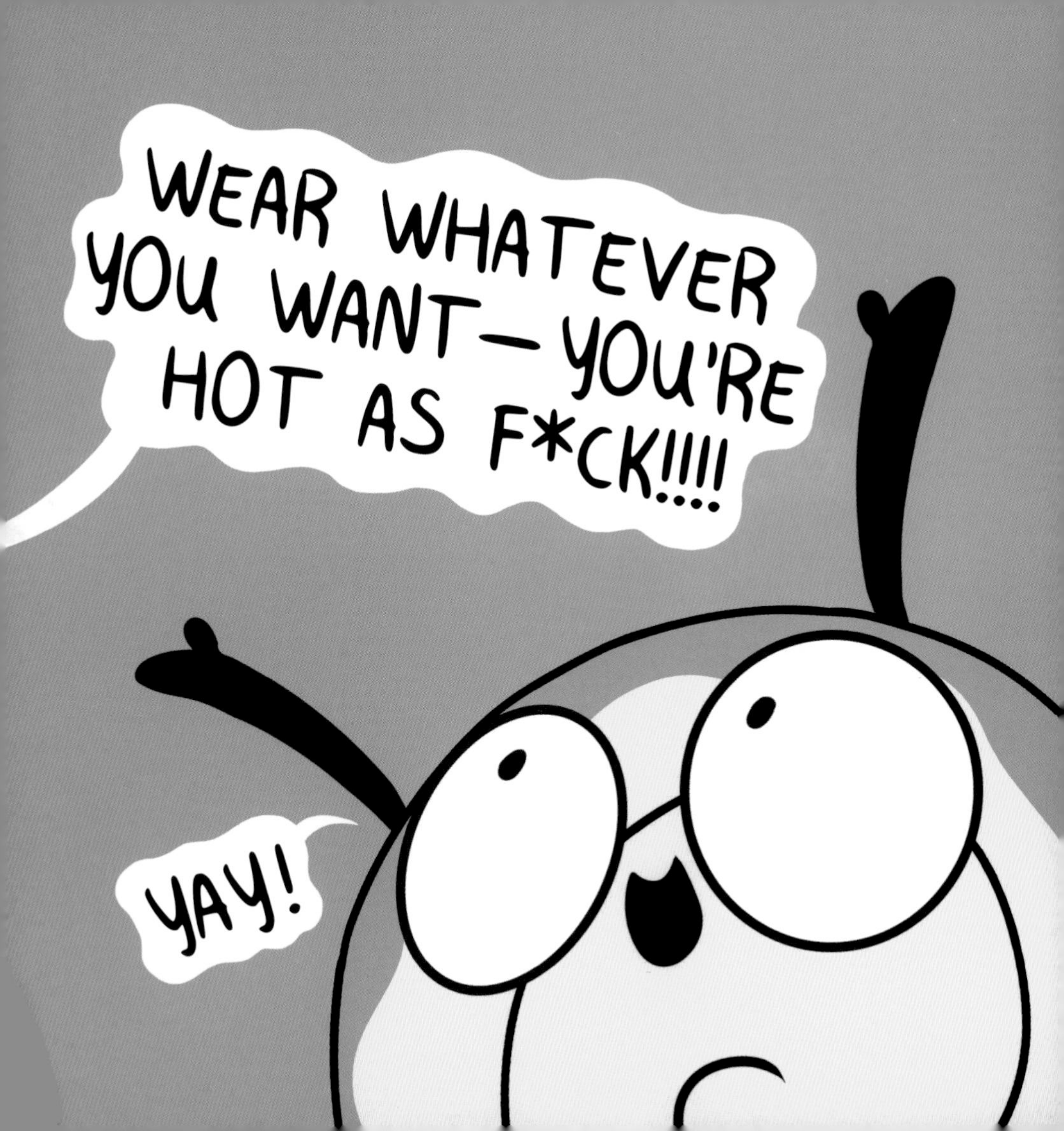
WEAR WHATEVER YOU WANT—YOU'RE HOT AS F*CK!!!!
YAY!

BODY ACCEPTANCE

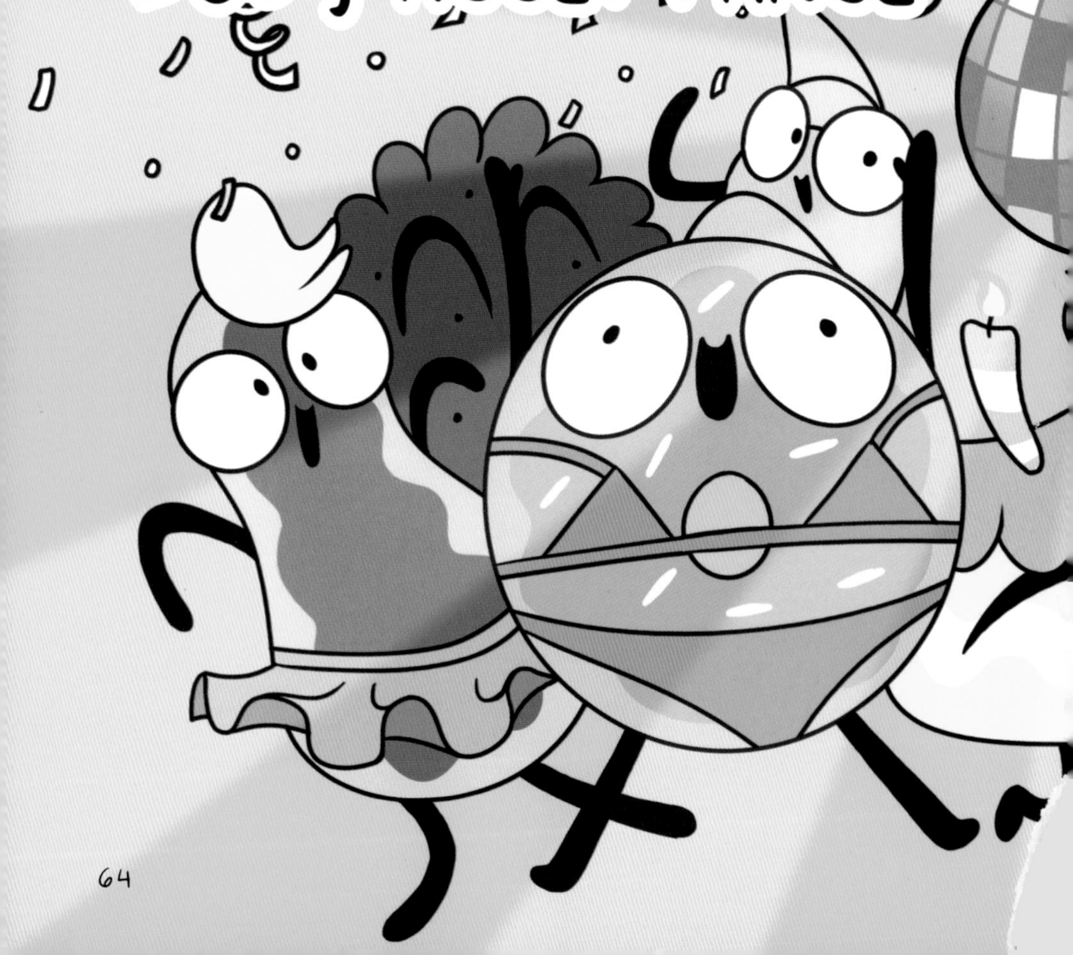

SELF-CARE: TAKE. MORE. NAPS.

IT IS EXTREMELY IMPORTANT
TO TAKE CARE OF YOURSELF.

THERE ARE MANY WAYS
TO DO THIS...

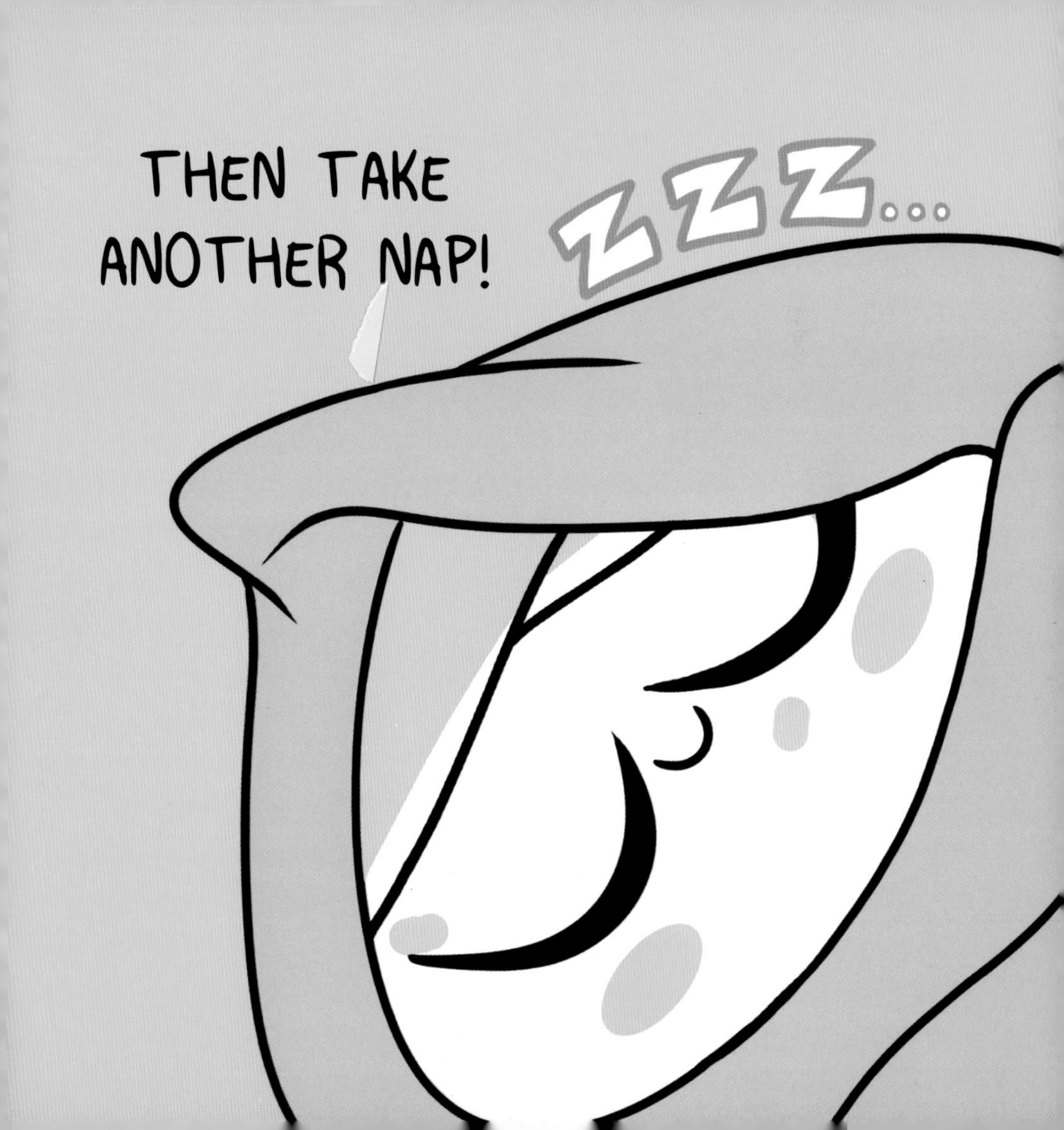
THEN TAKE ANOTHER NAP!
ZZZ...

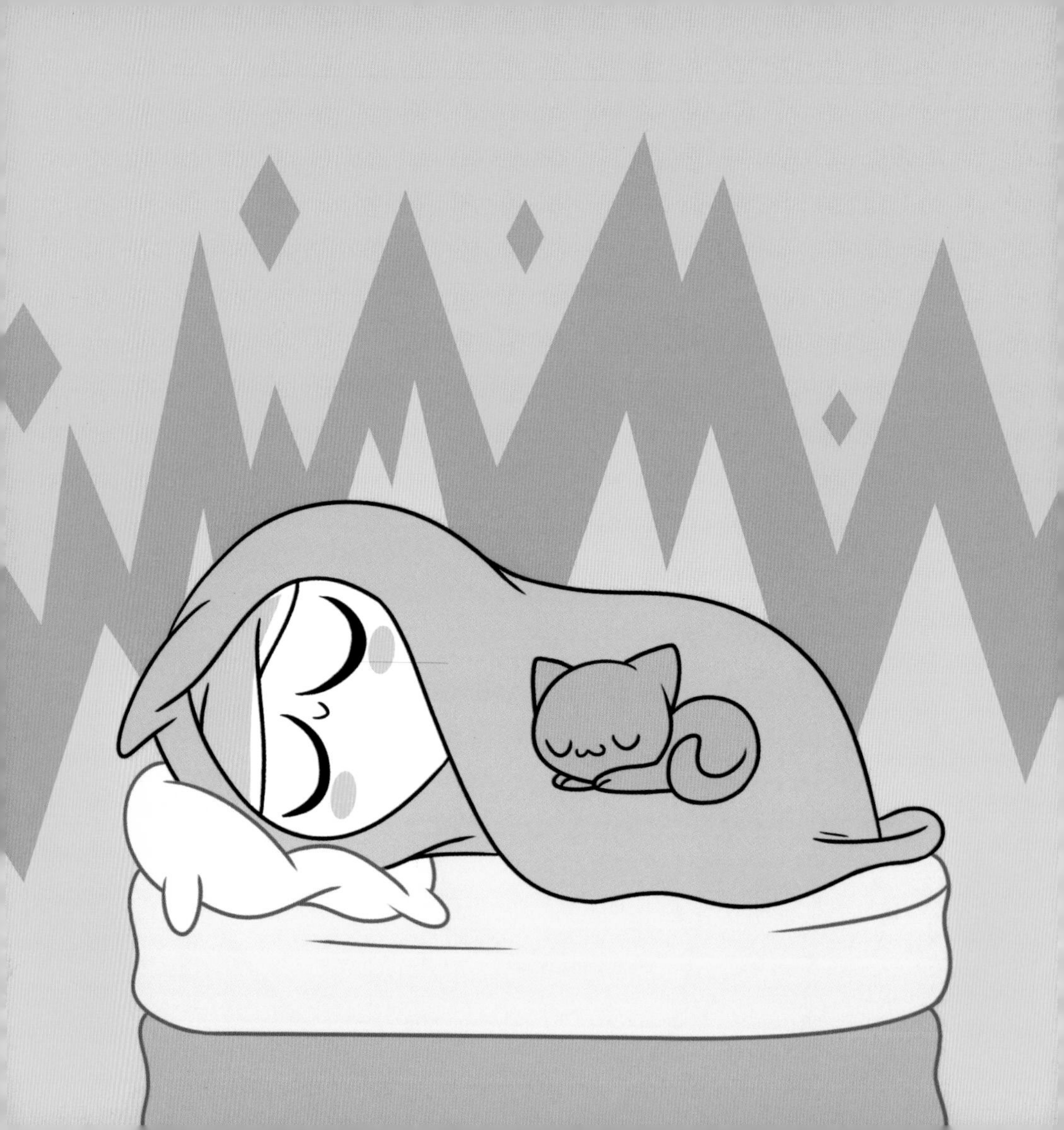

NAP THROUGH ALL THE
STRESS IN YOUR LIFE
UNTIL IT PASSES!

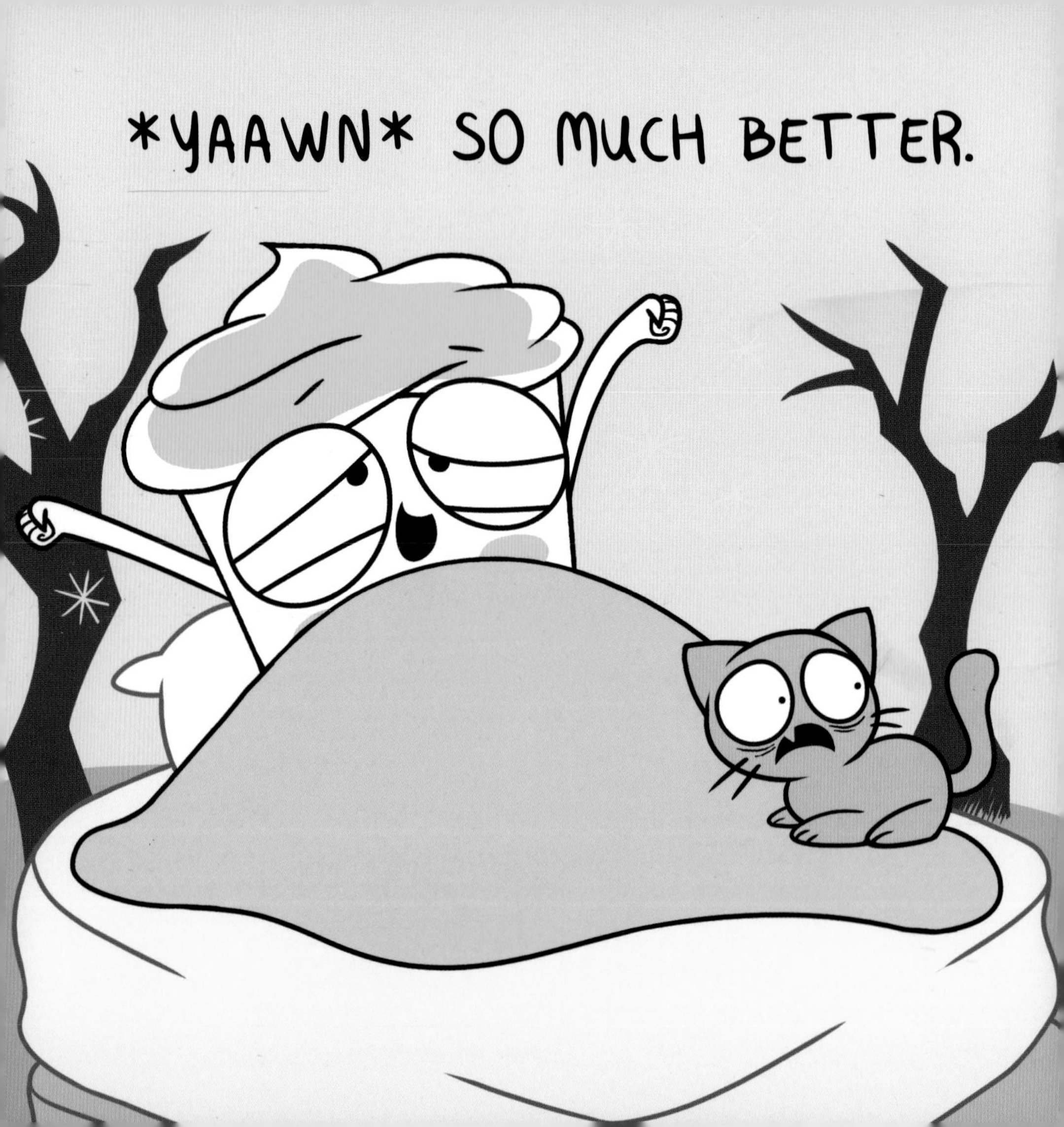
YAAWN SO MUCH BETTER.

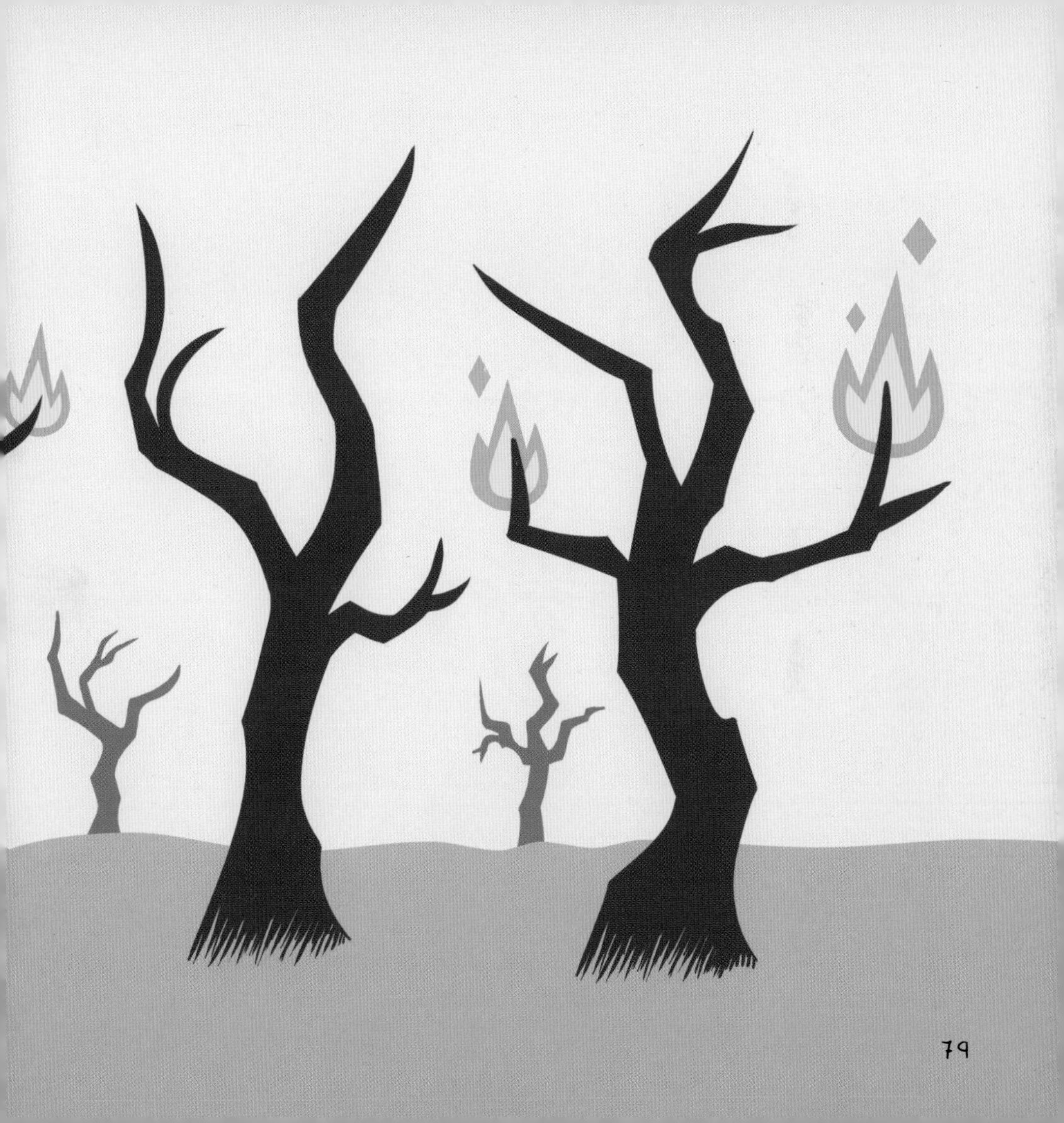

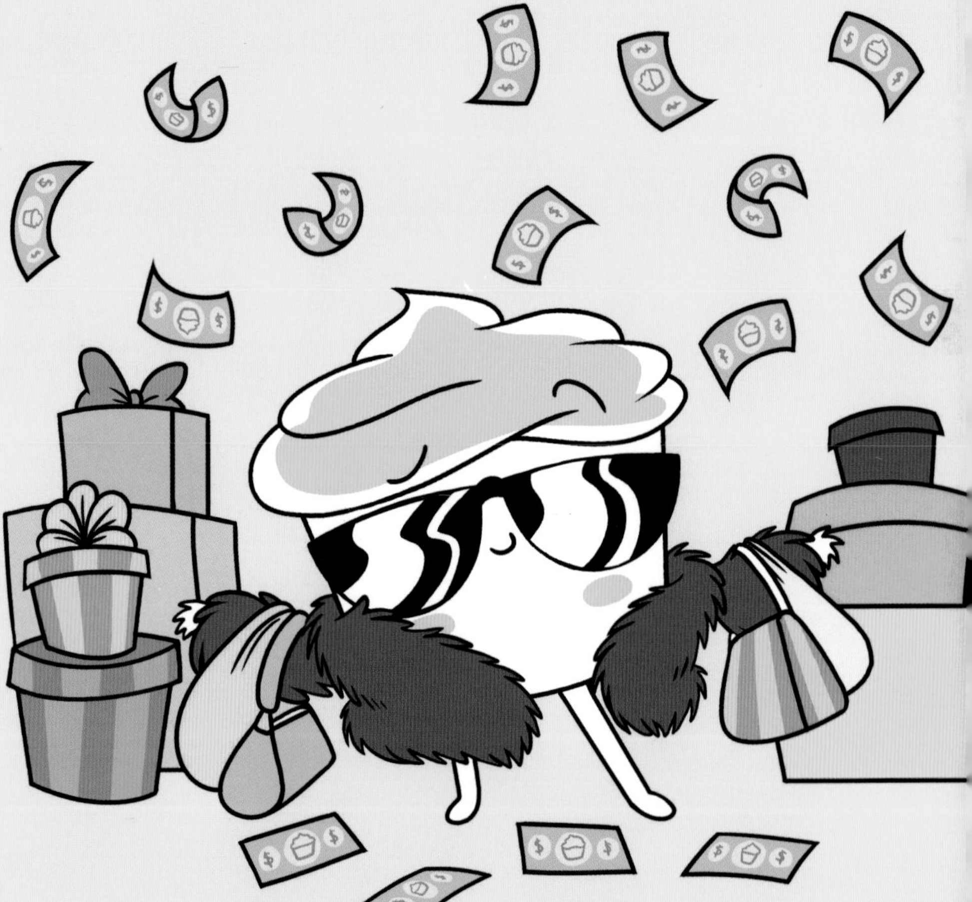

MONEY:
IT ISN'T
EVERYTHING,
BUT IT'S
SOMETHING

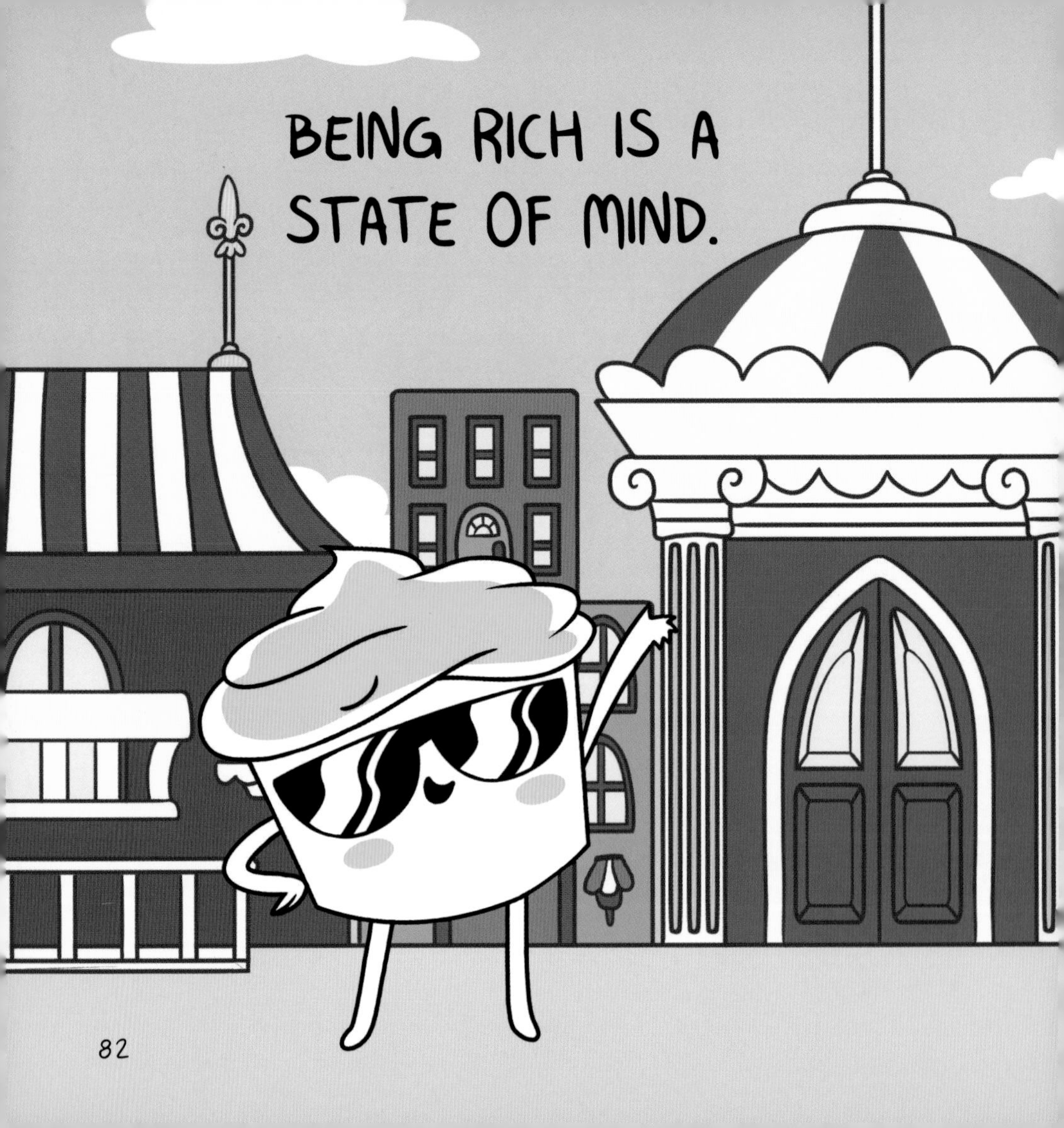
BEING RICH IS A STATE OF MIND.

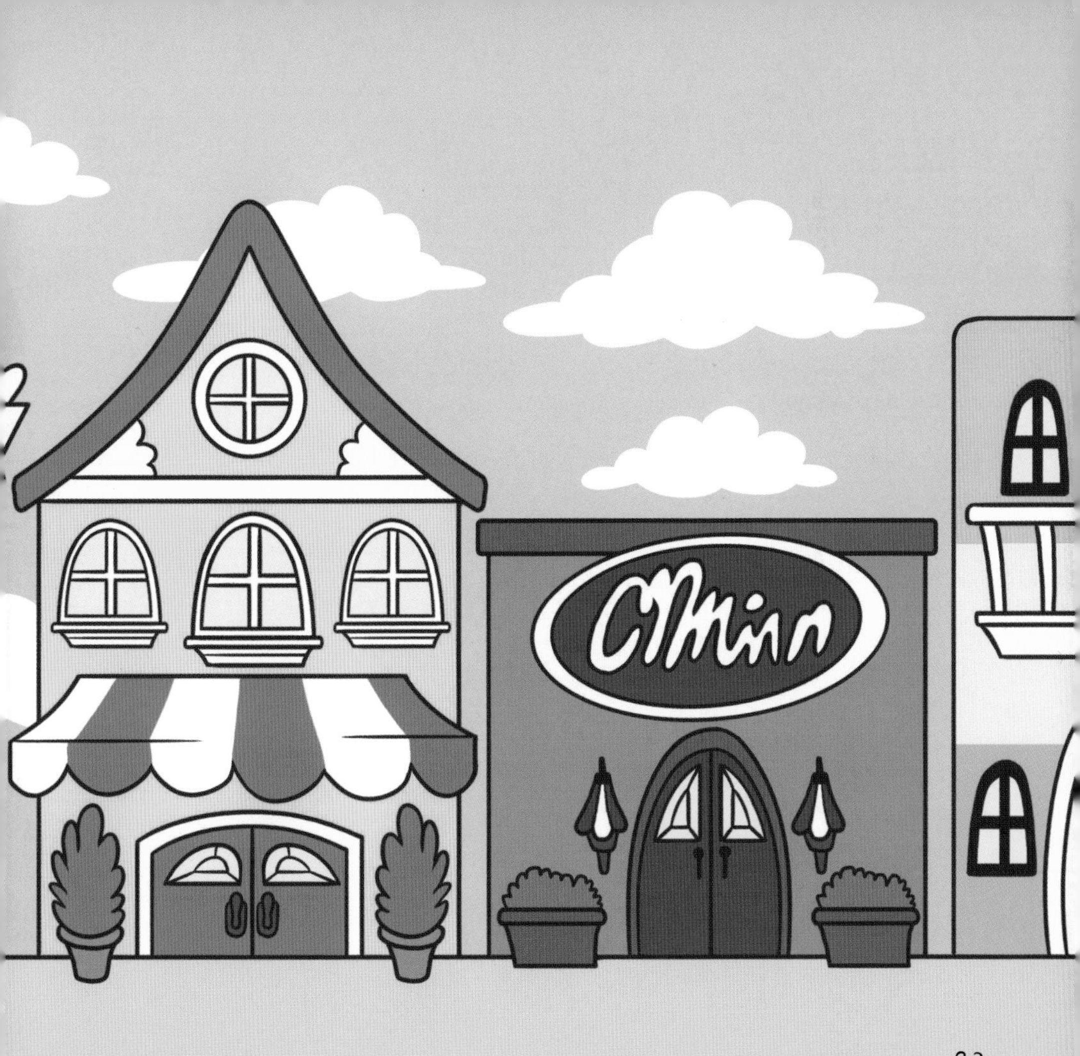

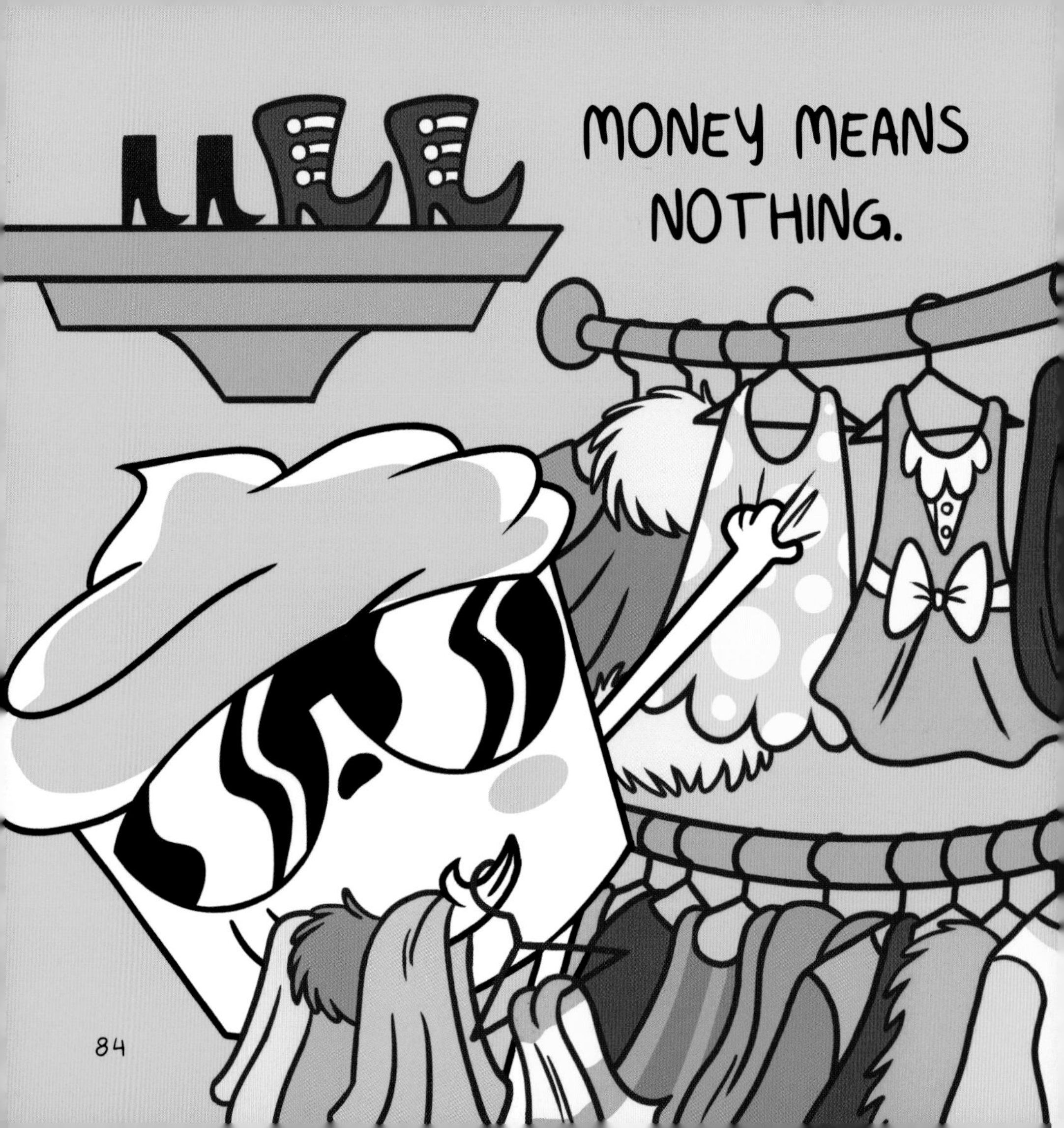
MONEY MEANS NOTHING.

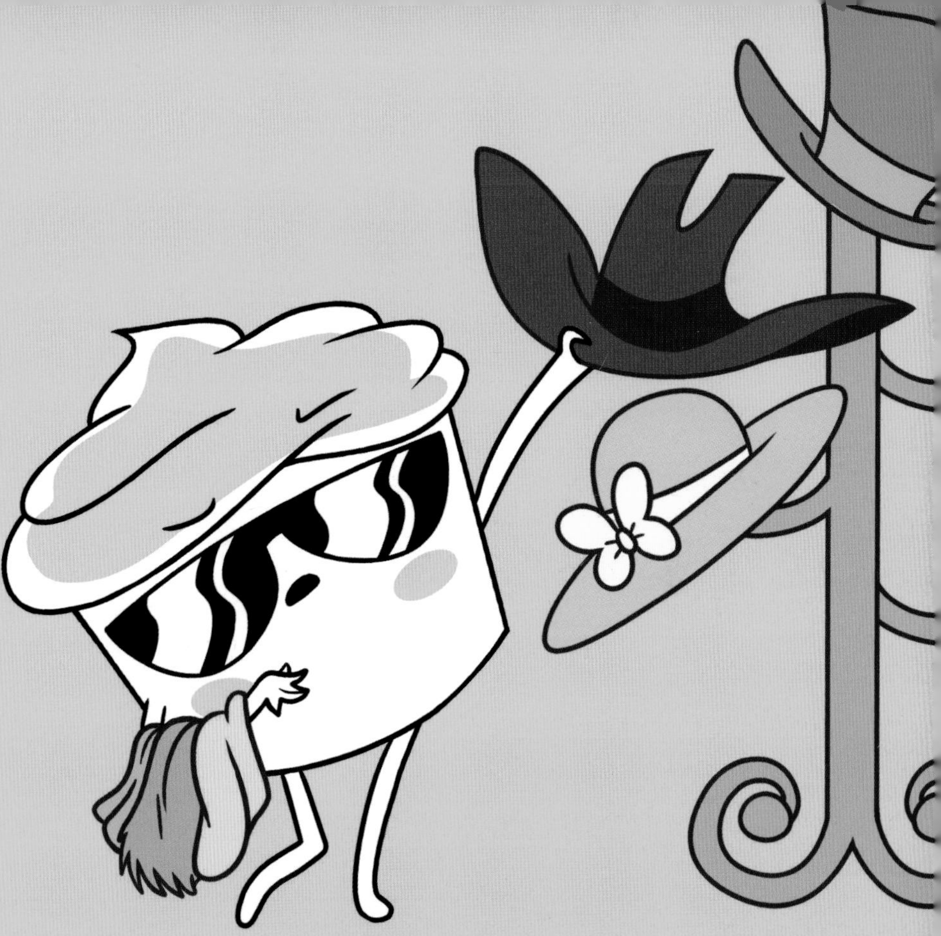

IT'S NOT IMPORTANT...

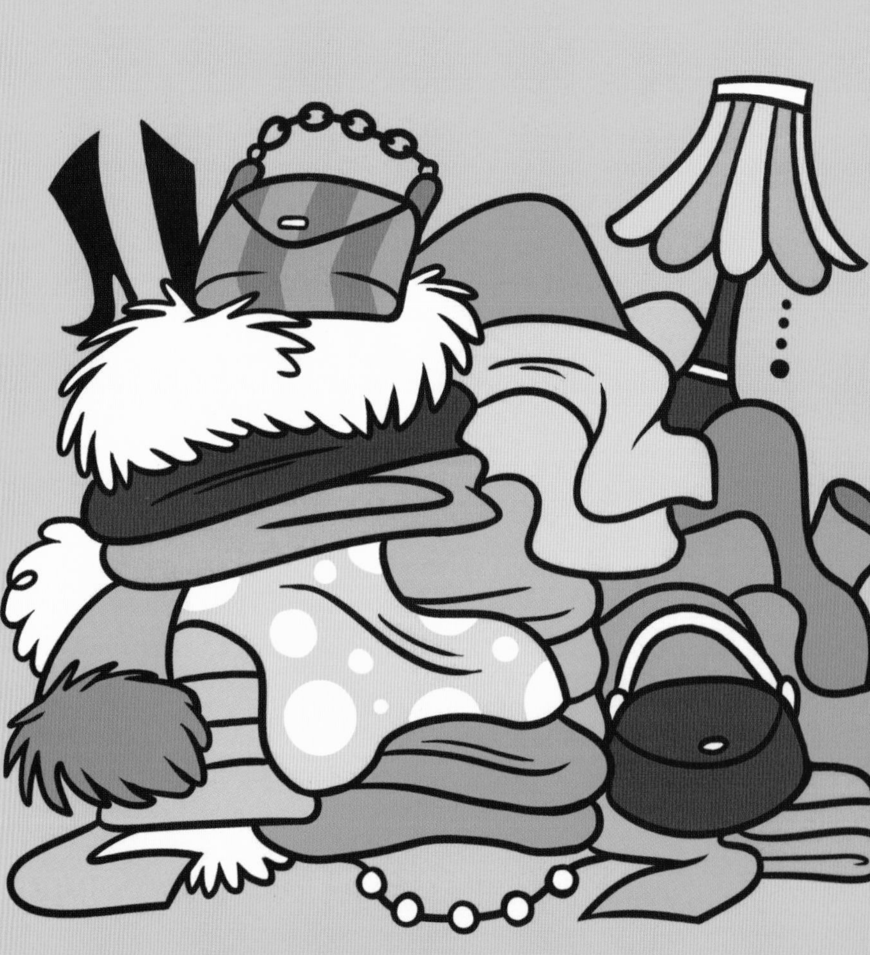

LOVE IS THE MOST IMPORTANT THING.

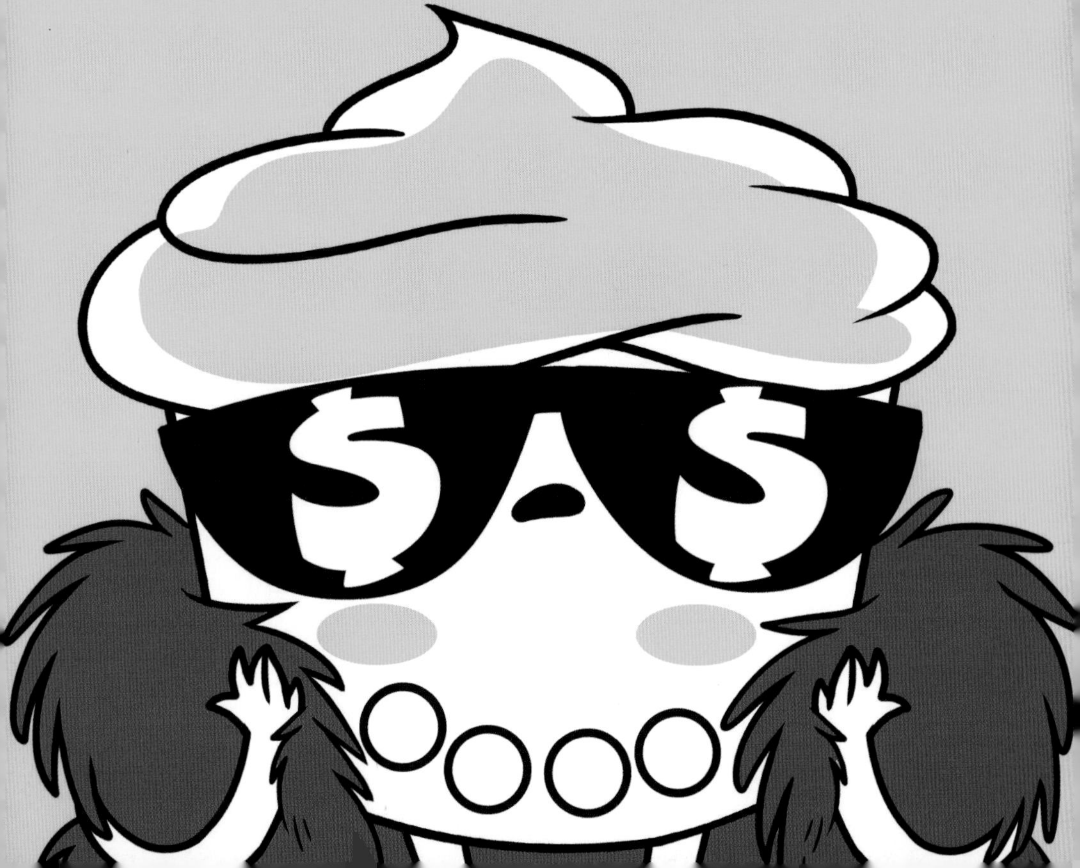

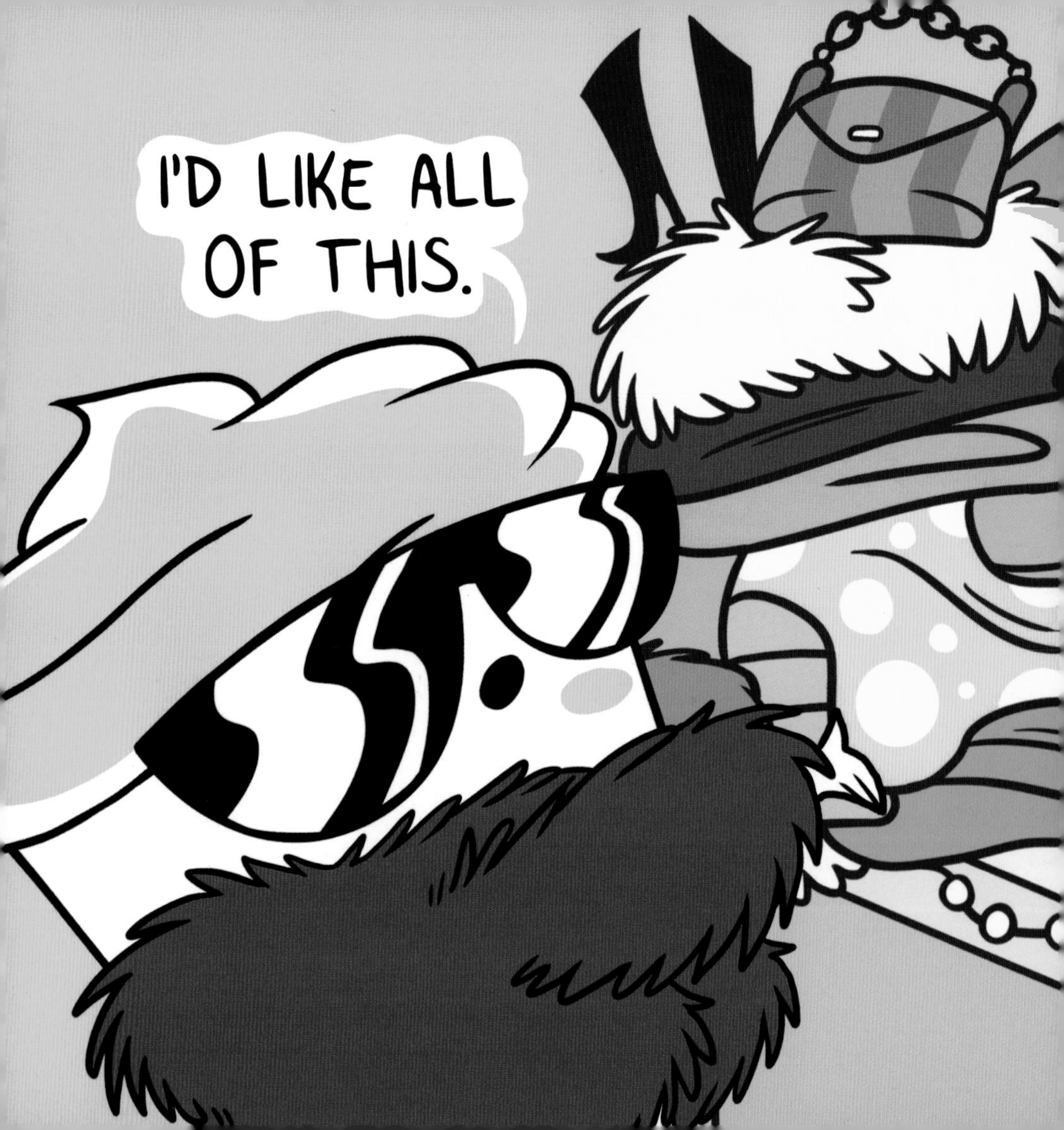
I'D LIKE ALL OF THIS.

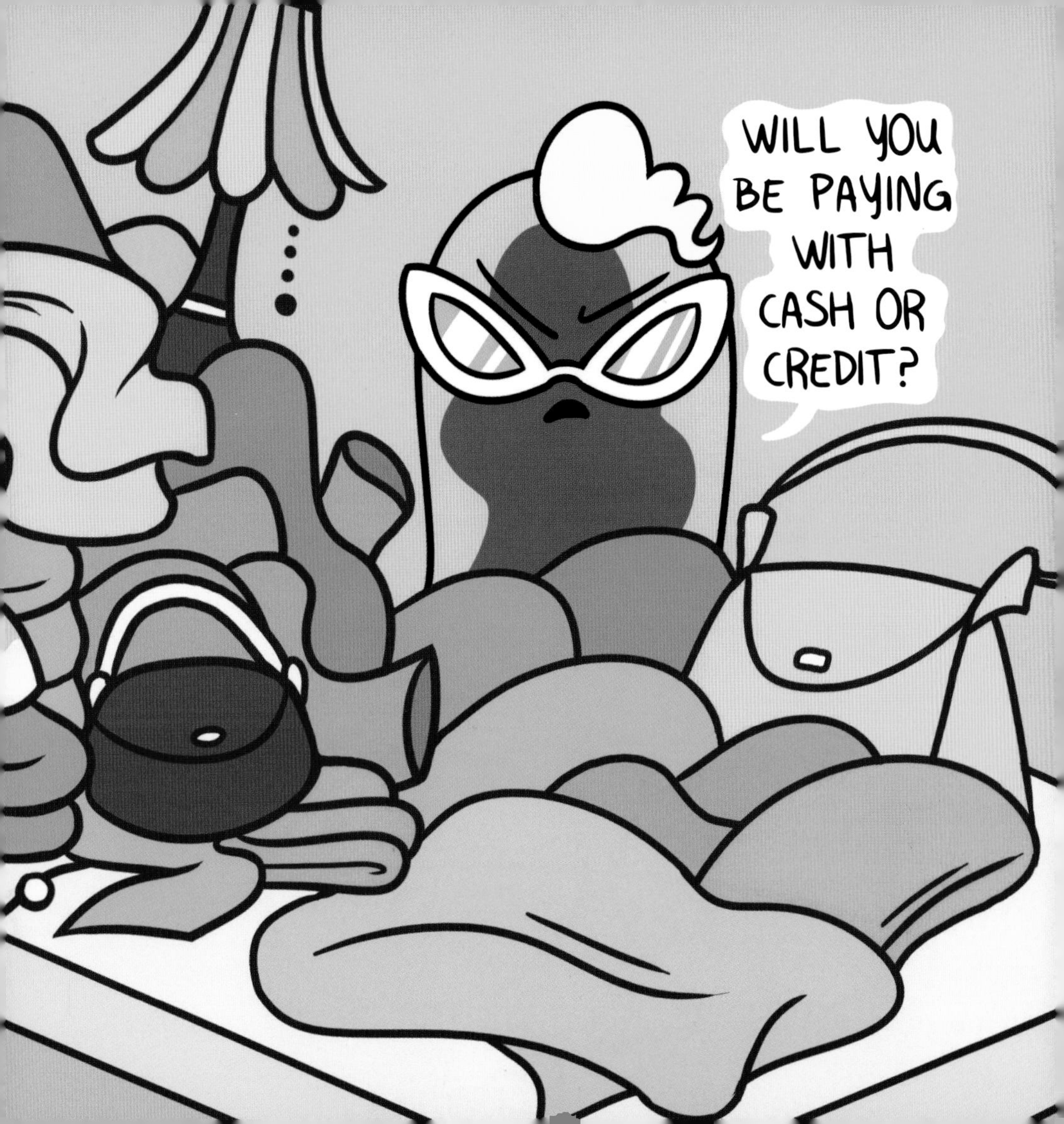
WILL YOU BE PAYING WITH CASH OR CREDIT?

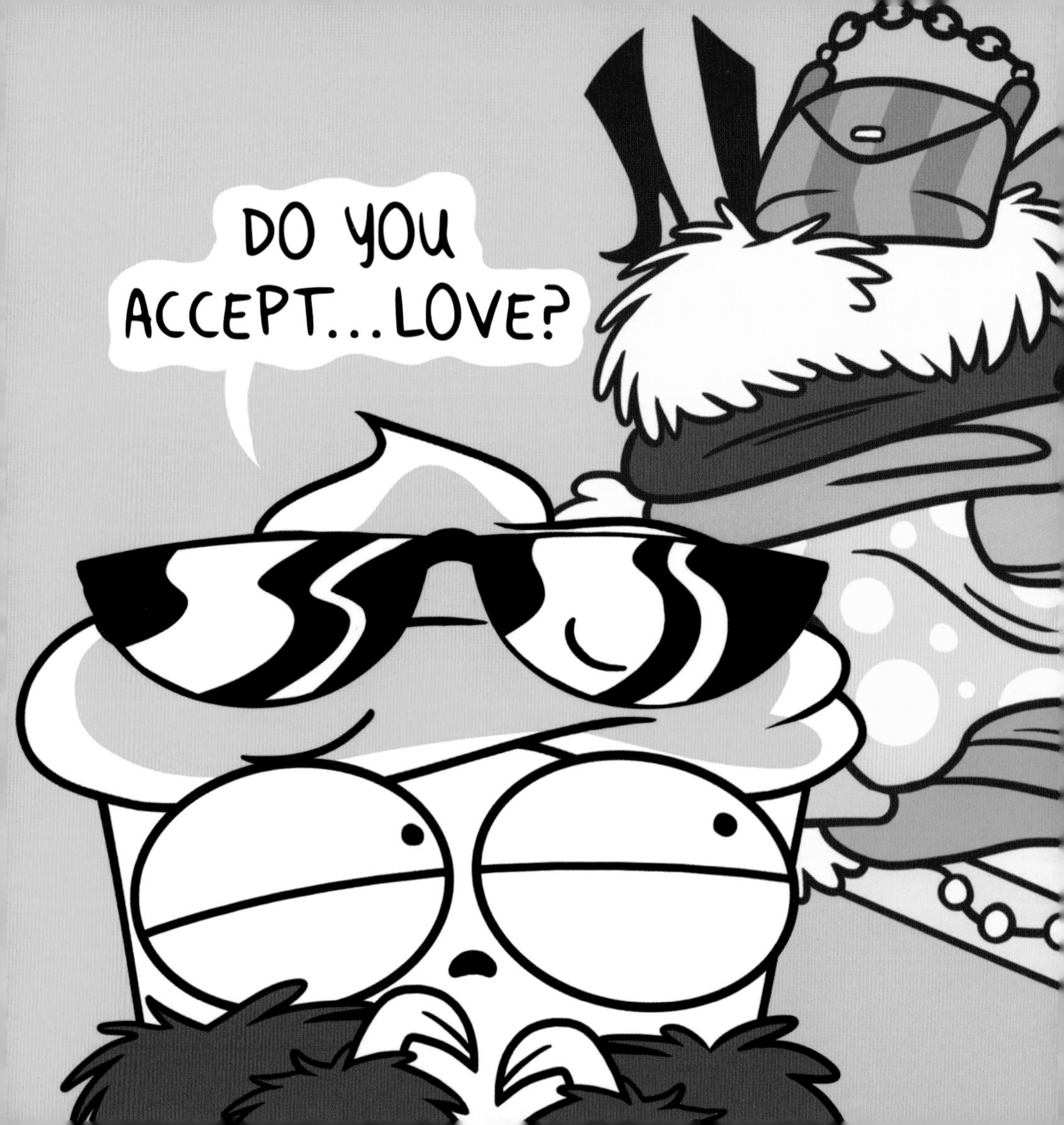
DO YOU
ACCEPT...LOVE?

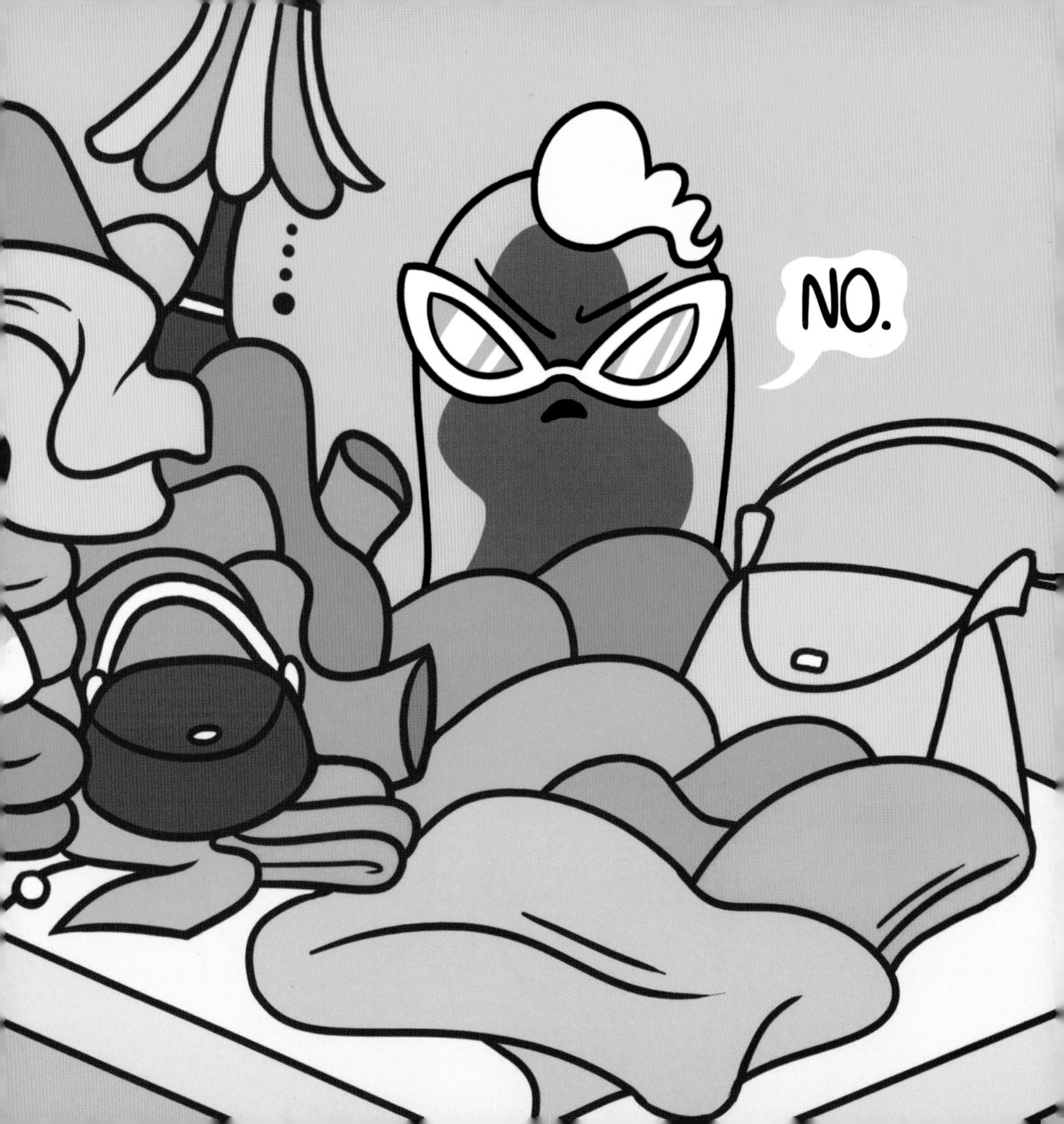
NO.

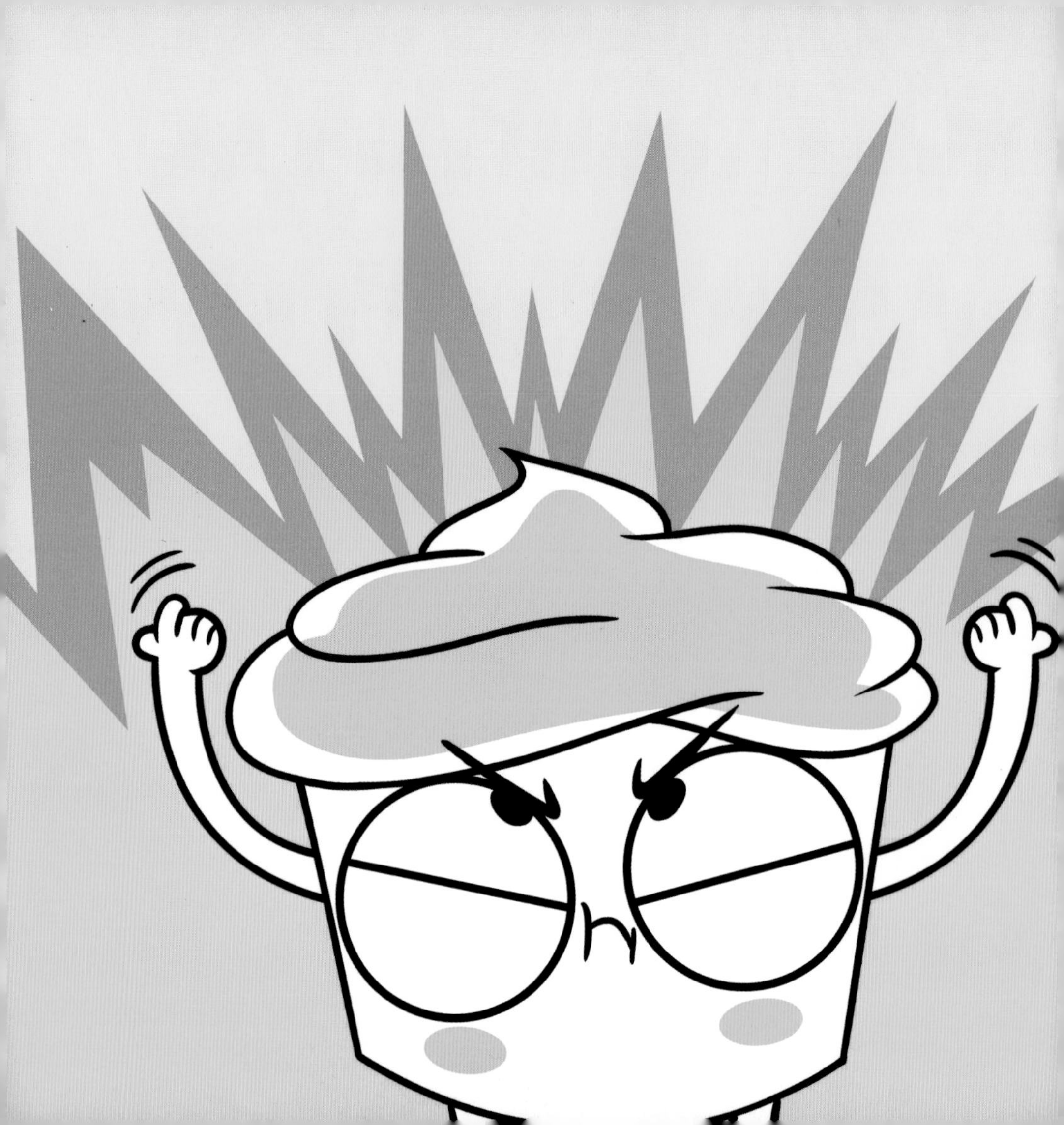

LIFE: GRAB IT BY THE BALLS!

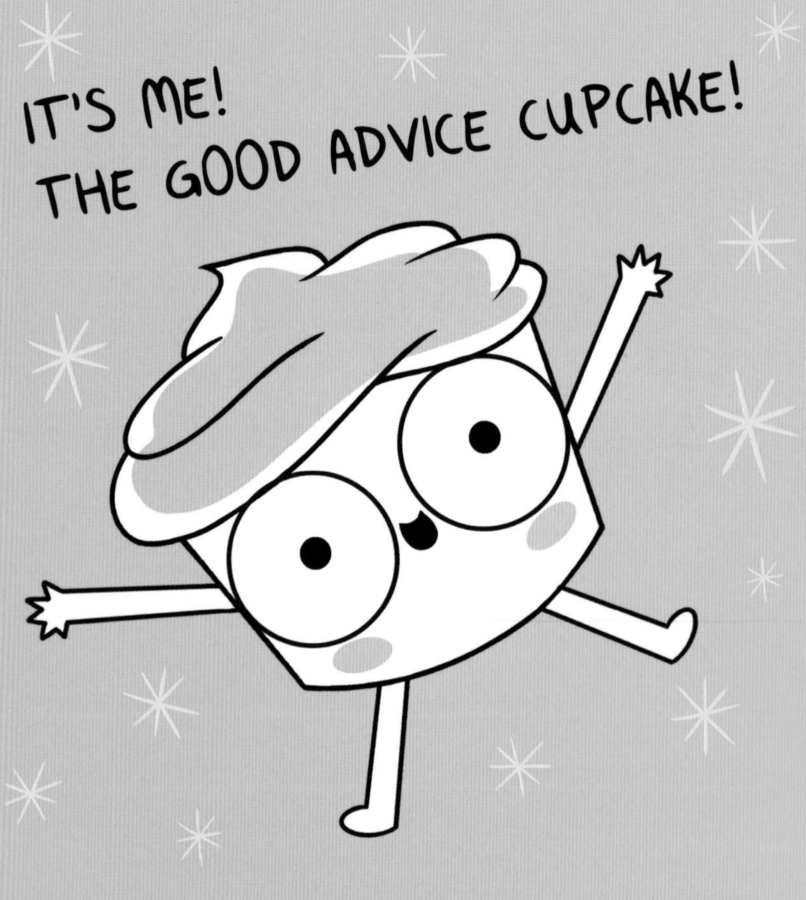
IT'S ME!
THE GOOD ADVICE CUPCAKE!

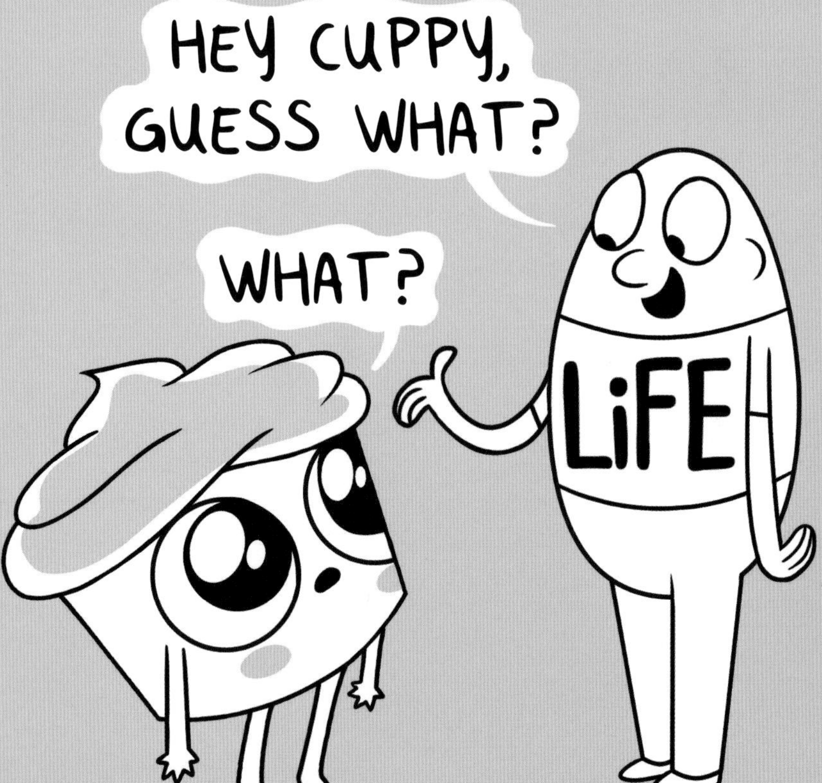
HEY CUPPY,
GUESS WHAT?
WHAT?
LiFE

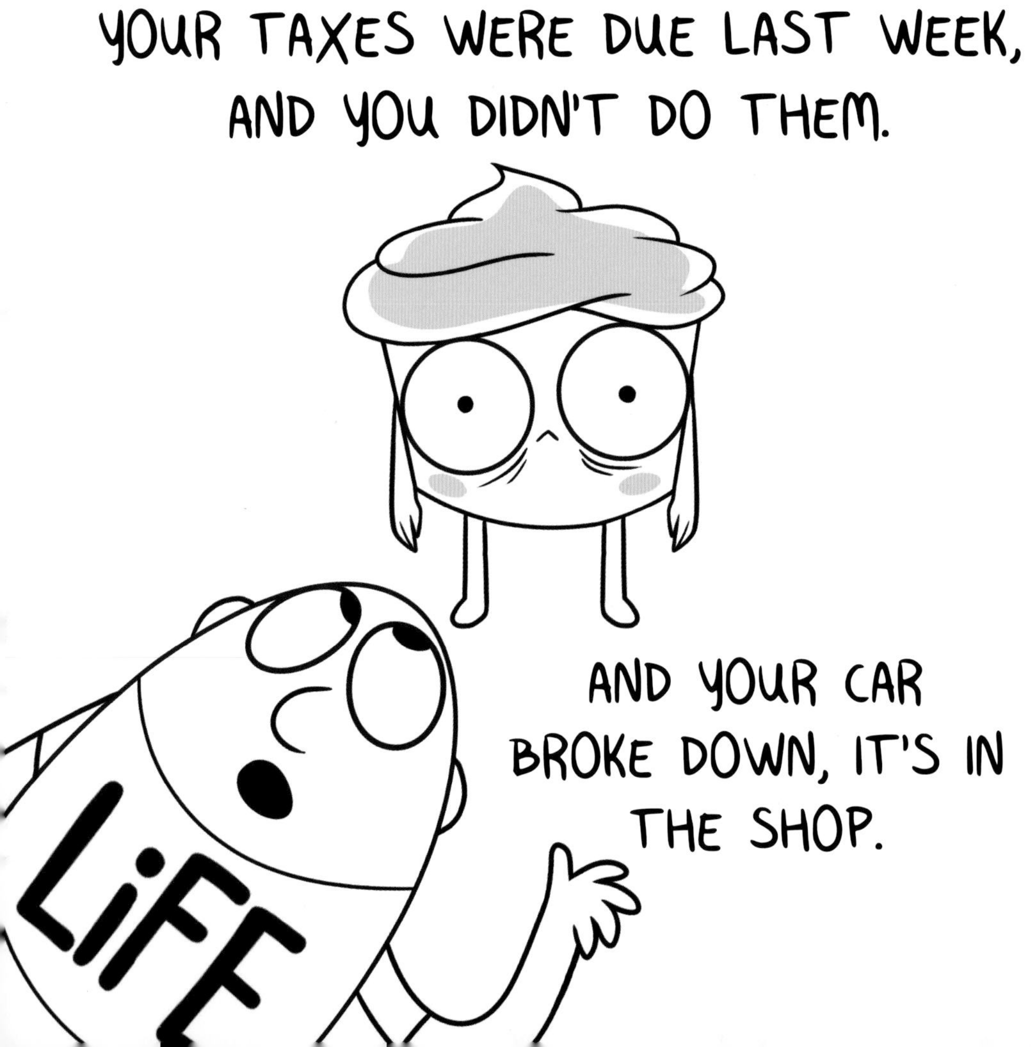
YOUR TAXES WERE DUE LAST WEEK, AND YOU DIDN'T DO THEM.
AND YOUR CAR BROKE DOWN, IT'S IN THE SHOP.
LIFE

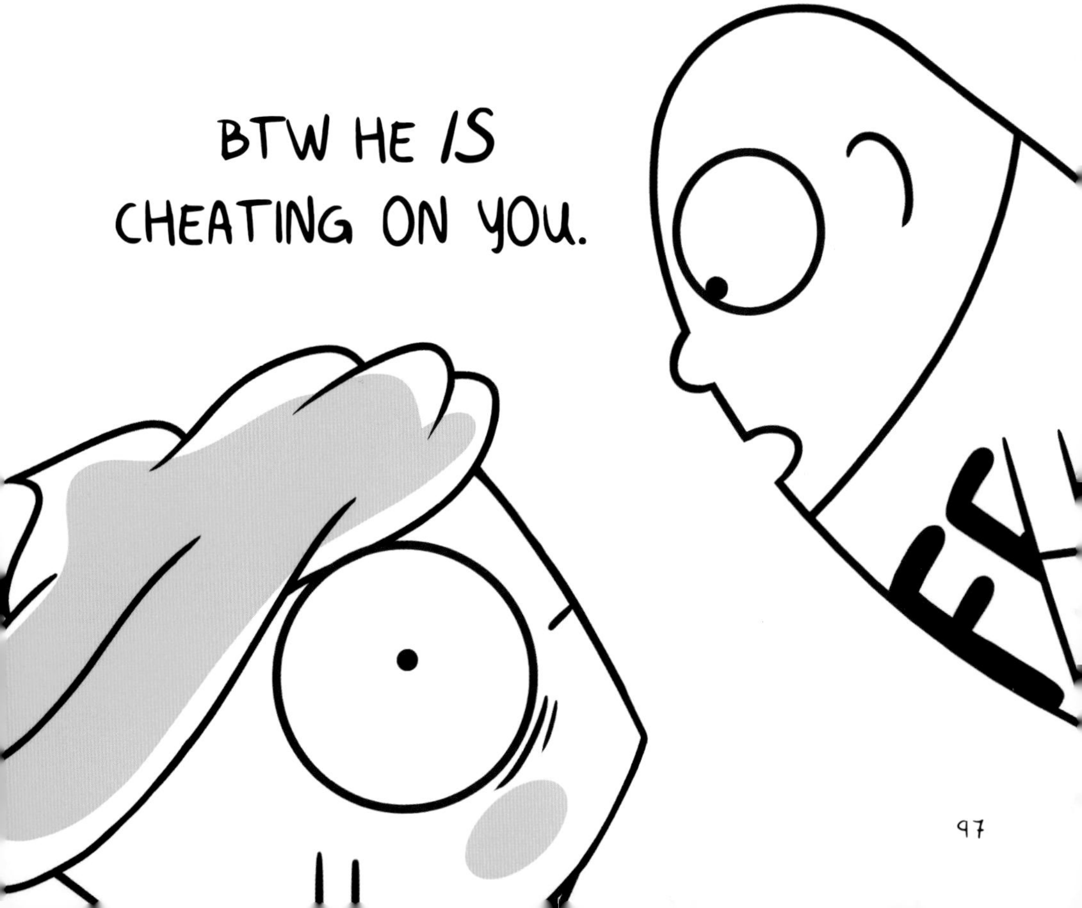
BTW HE IS
CHEATING ON YOU.

ALSO, YOUR CAT SPRINKLES HAS A FEVER.

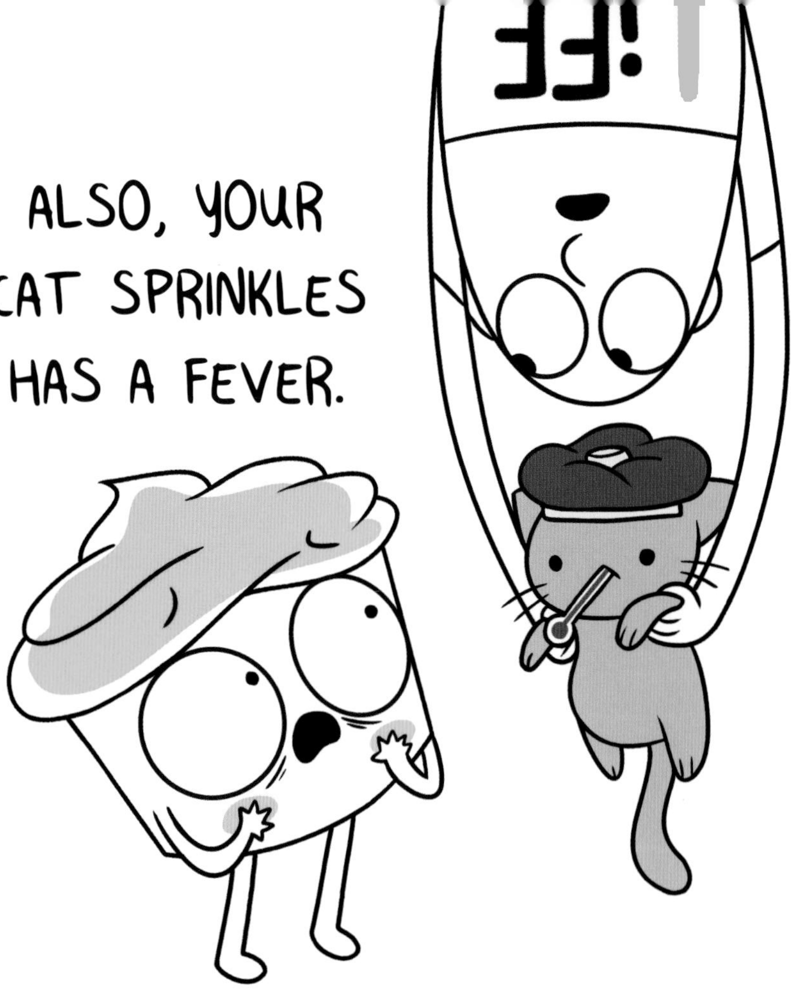

SOMETIMES LIFE
CAN BE A REAL JERK!

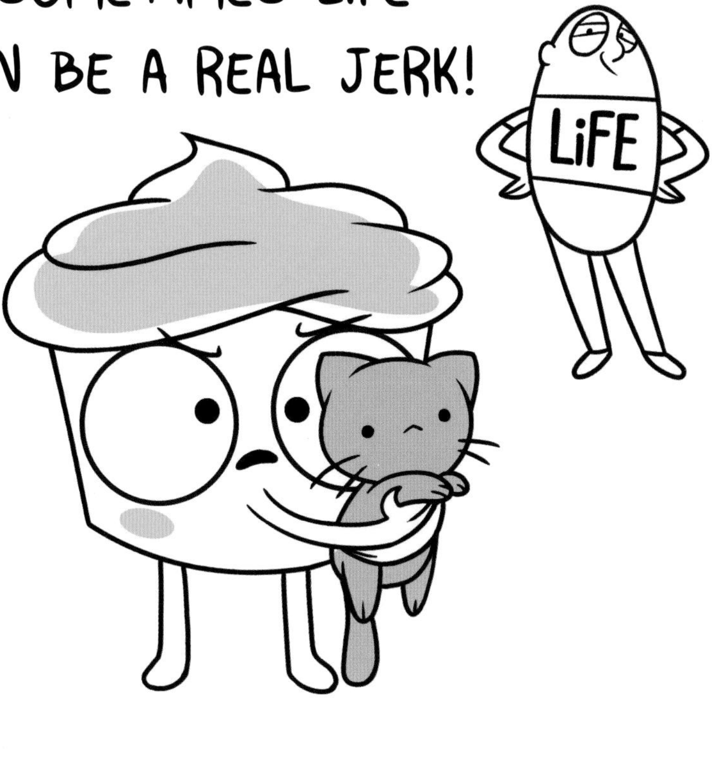
LiFE

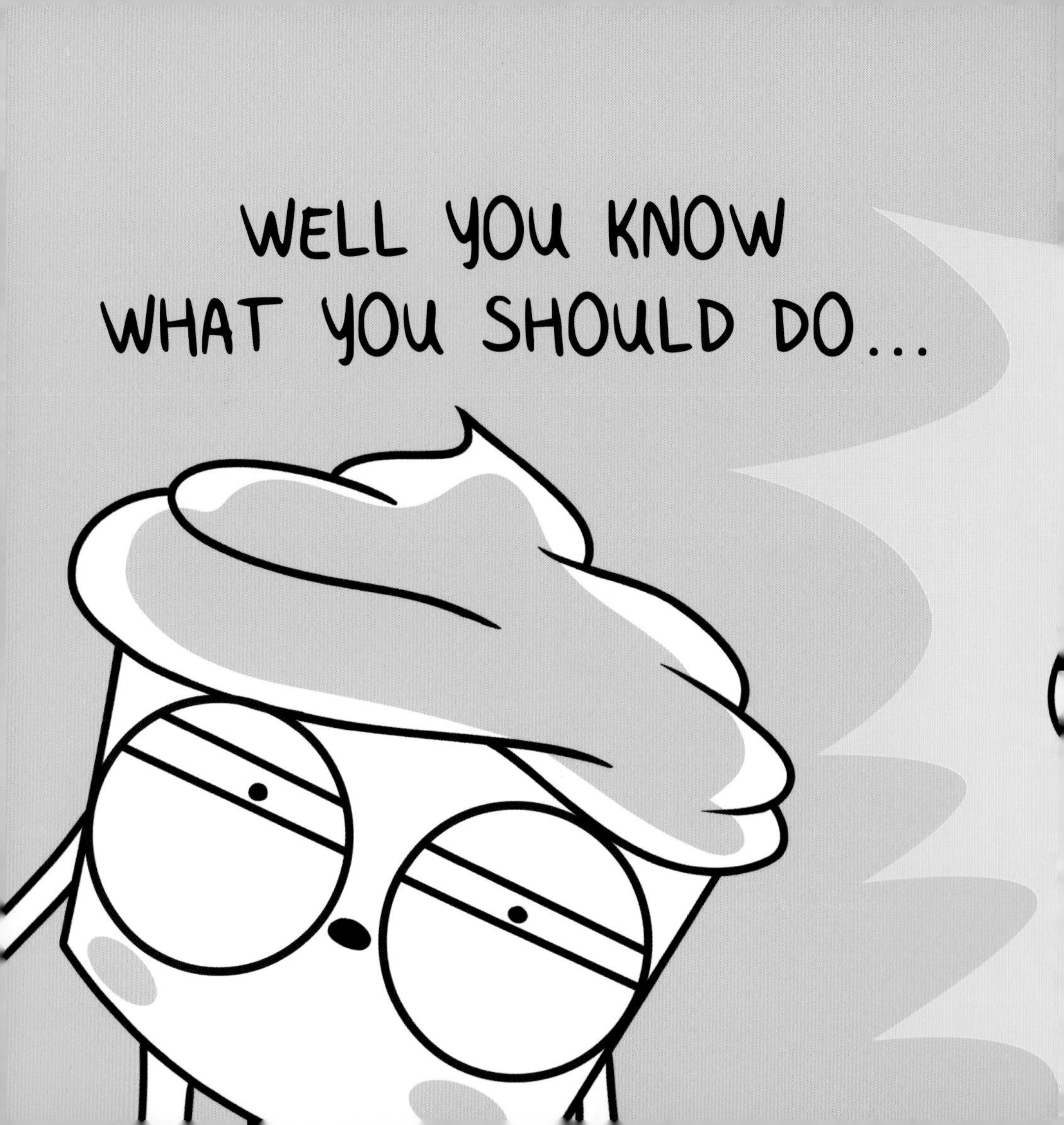
WELL YOU KNOW
WHAT YOU SHOULD DO...

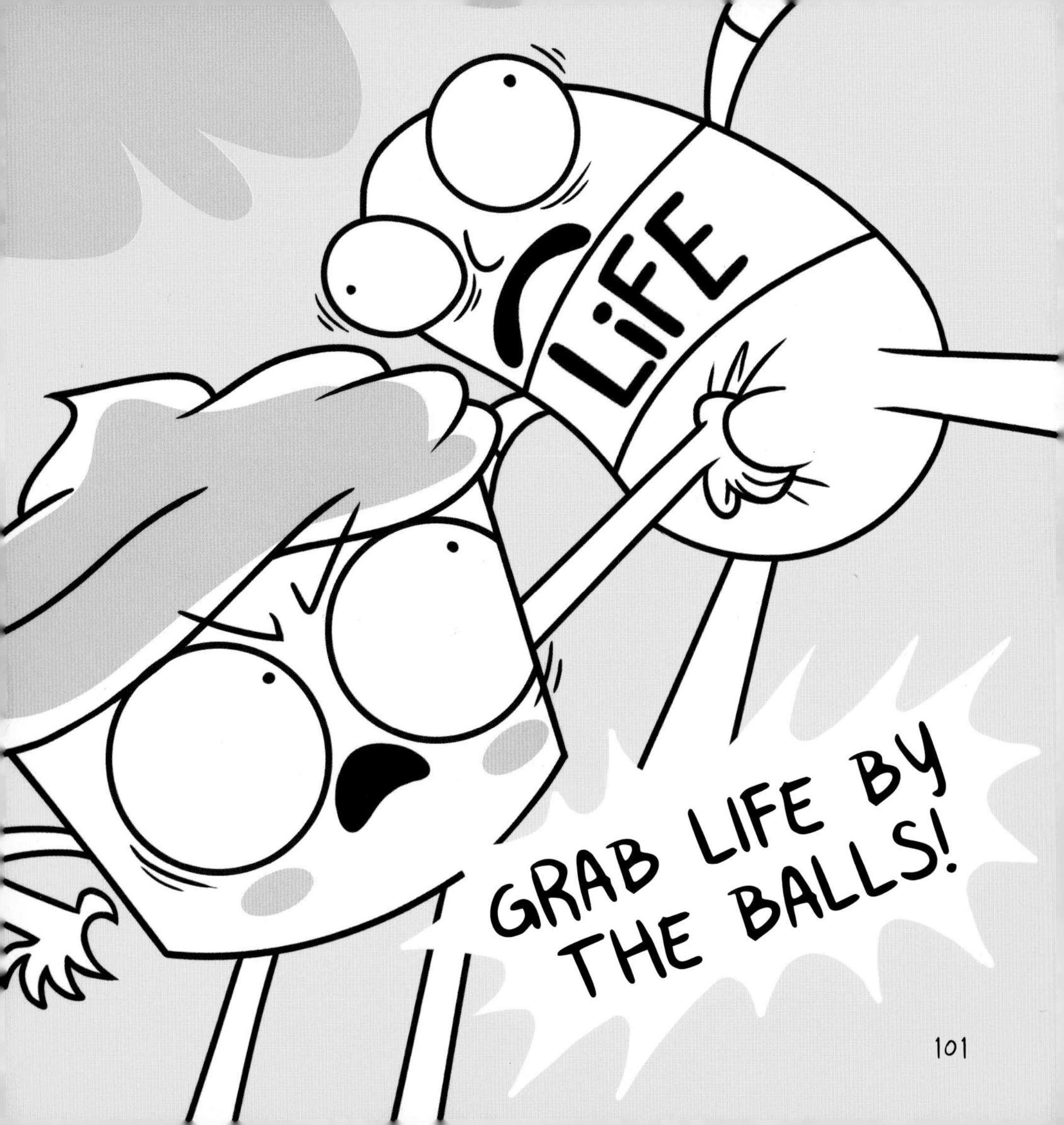
LiFE
GRAB LIFE BY THE BALLS!

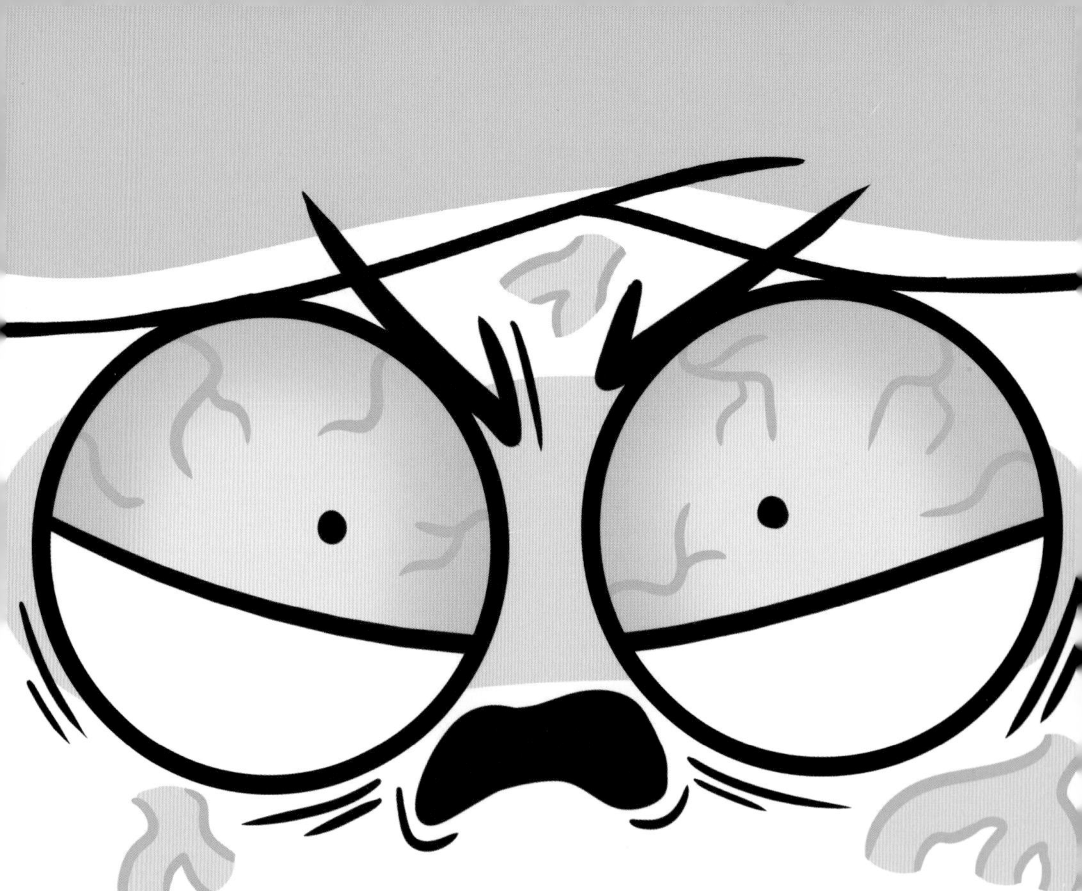

AND MAKE LIFE YOUR B*TCH!!!

OK OK, FINE, EVERYTHING WILL GET BETTER!

THAT'S RIGHT.

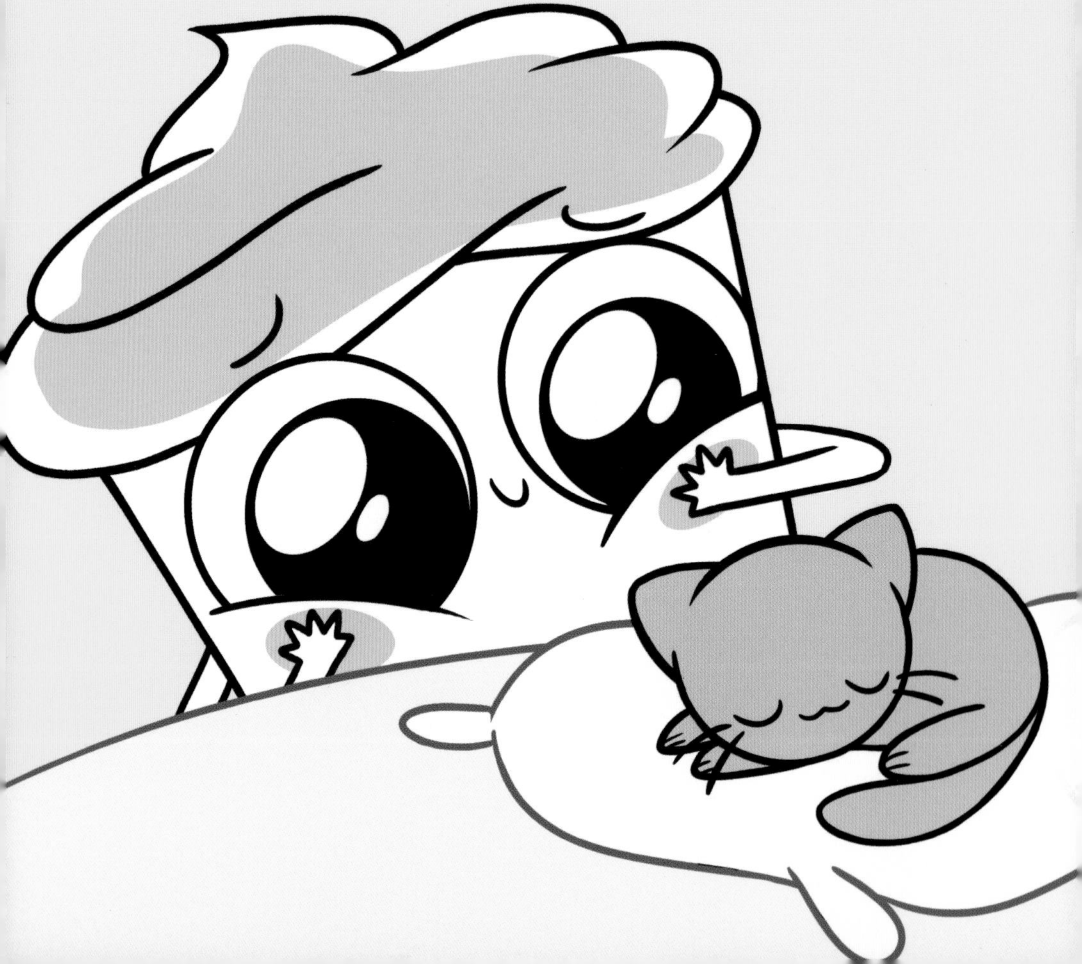

PET CARE: WINNING YOUR CAT'S AFFECTION

WHEN WINNING THE AFFECTION OF YOUR CAT, IT IS IMPORTANT TO NOT APPEAR TOO DESPERATE.

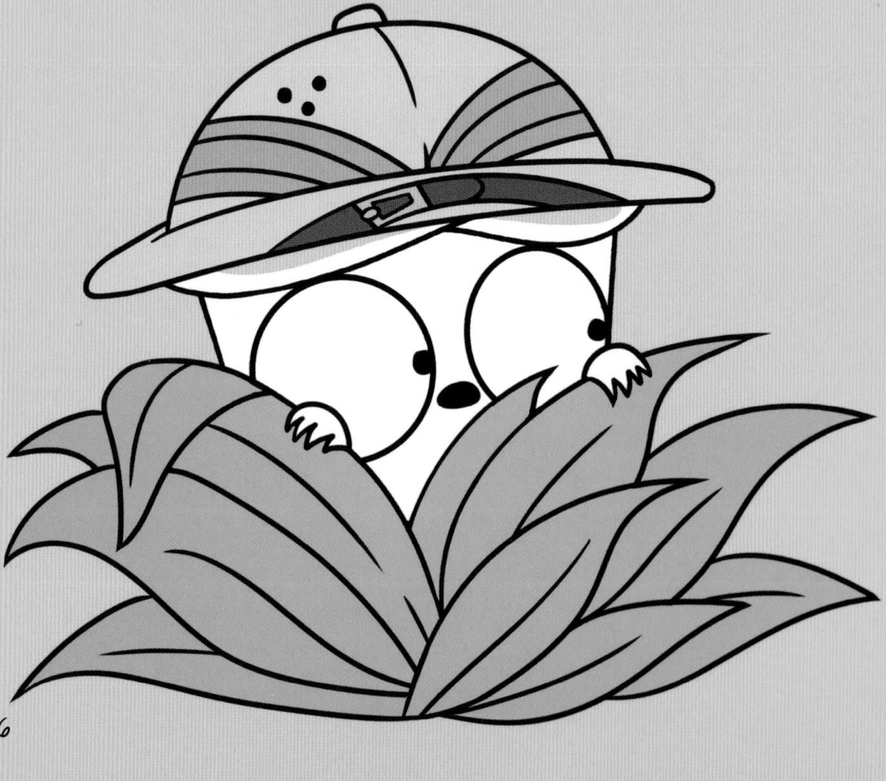

CATS CAN NATURALLY SMELL NEEDINESS AND IT REPELS THEM.

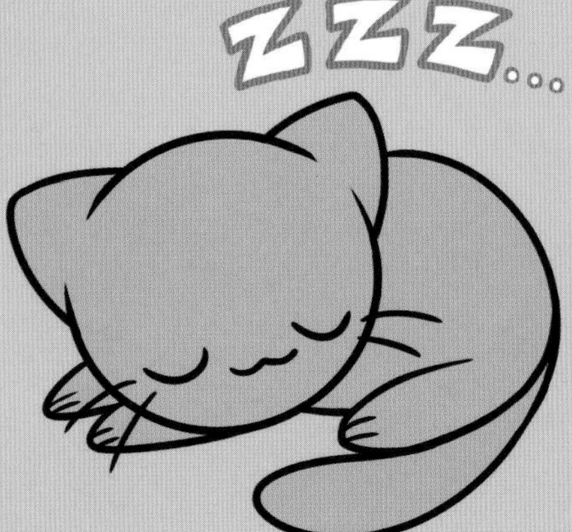
ZZZ...

BE SURE TO ACT COOL...

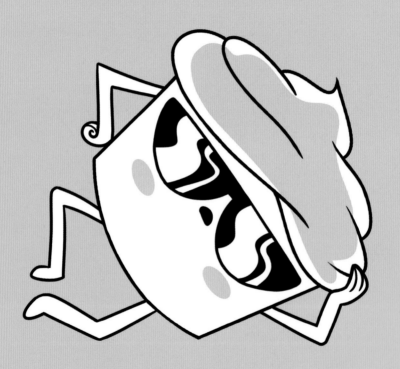

AND NOT STARE AT
THEM TOO MUCH...

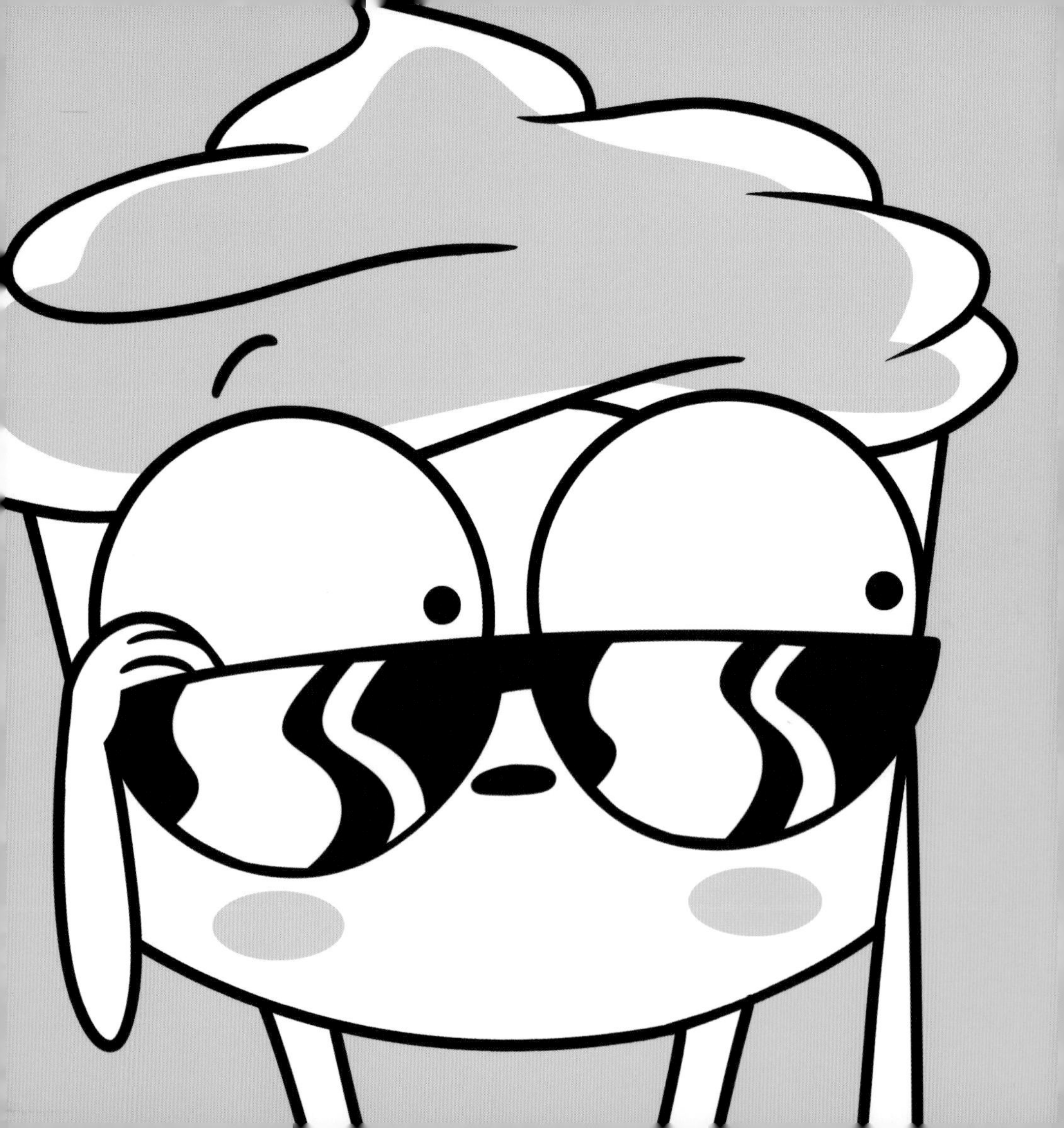

EVEN IF THEY ARE THE
CUTEST THING YOU'VE...
EVER SEEN...

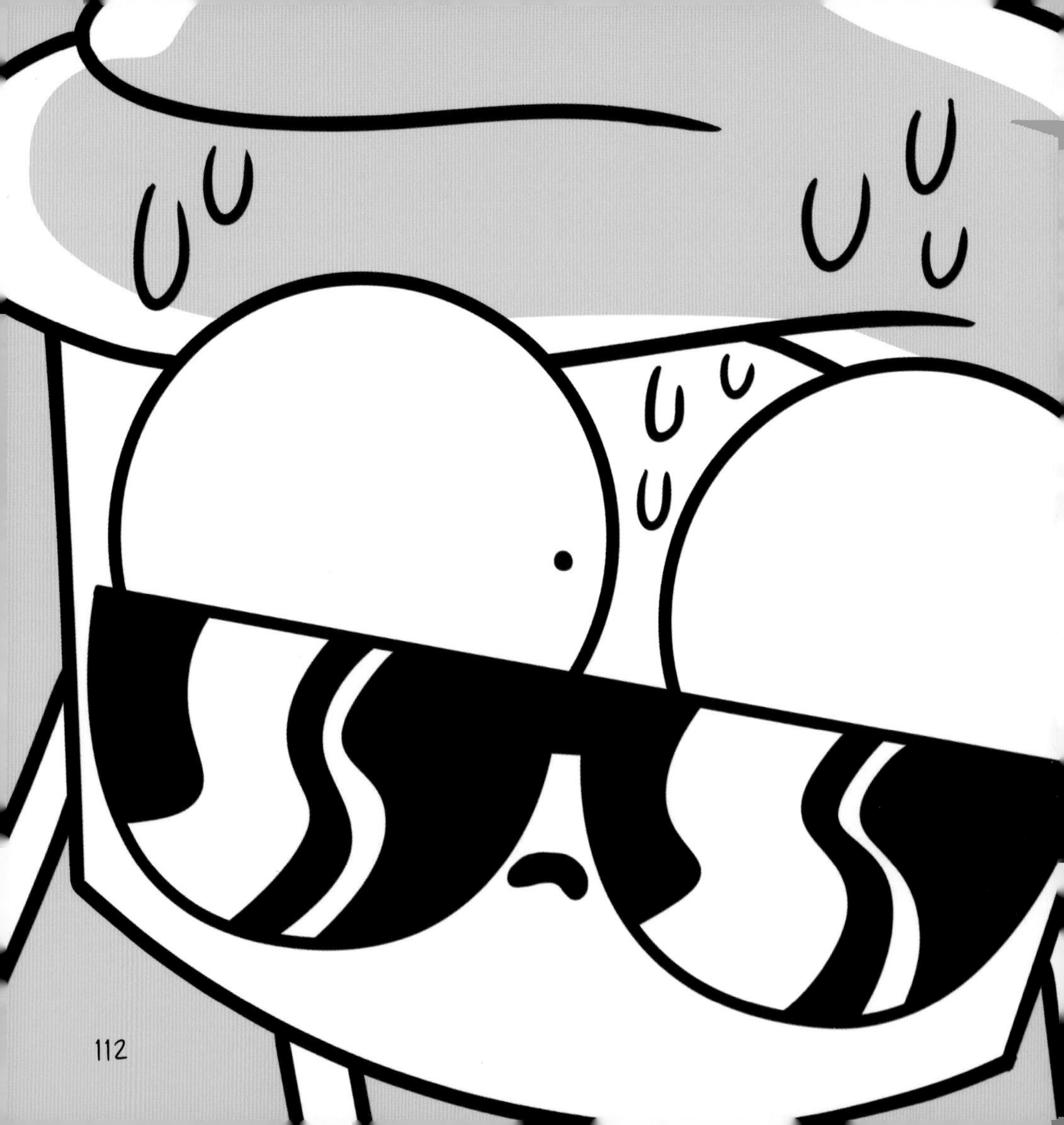

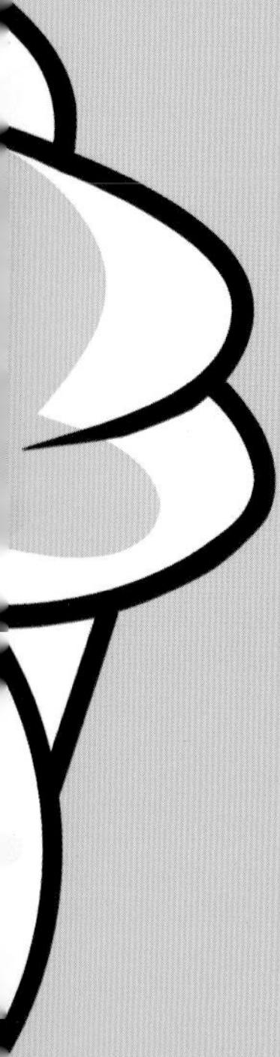

LET... YOUR CAT...
COME TO YOU...

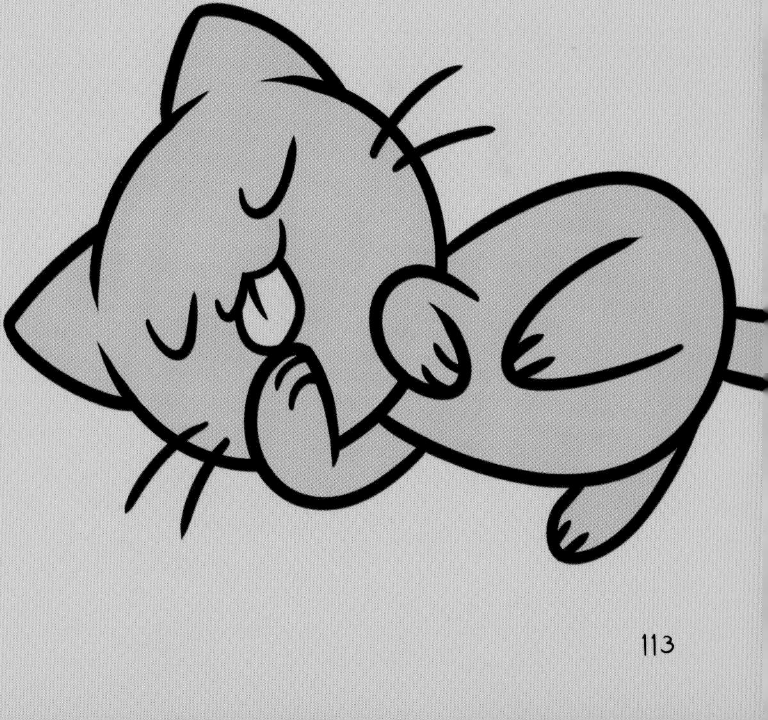

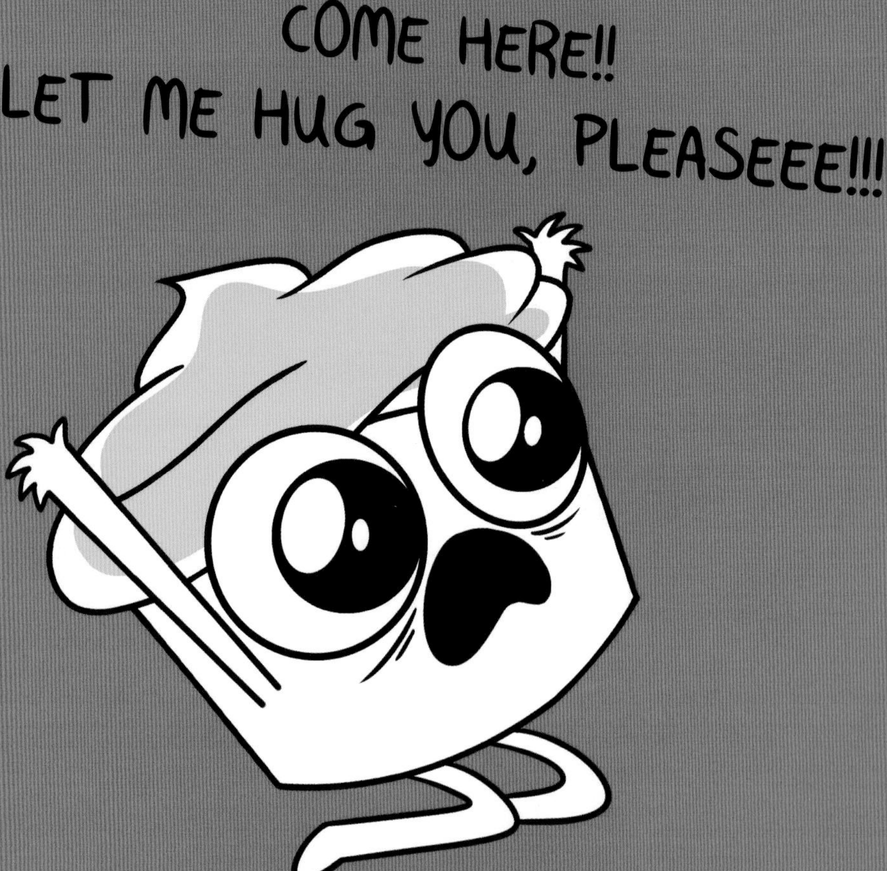
COME HERE!!
LET ME HUG YOU, PLEASEEE!!!

NOOOO, I LOVE YOU SO MUCH....

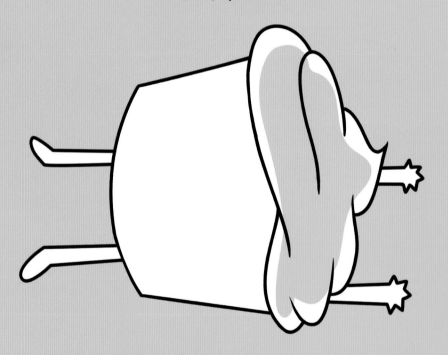

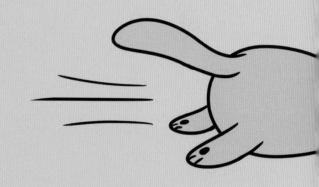

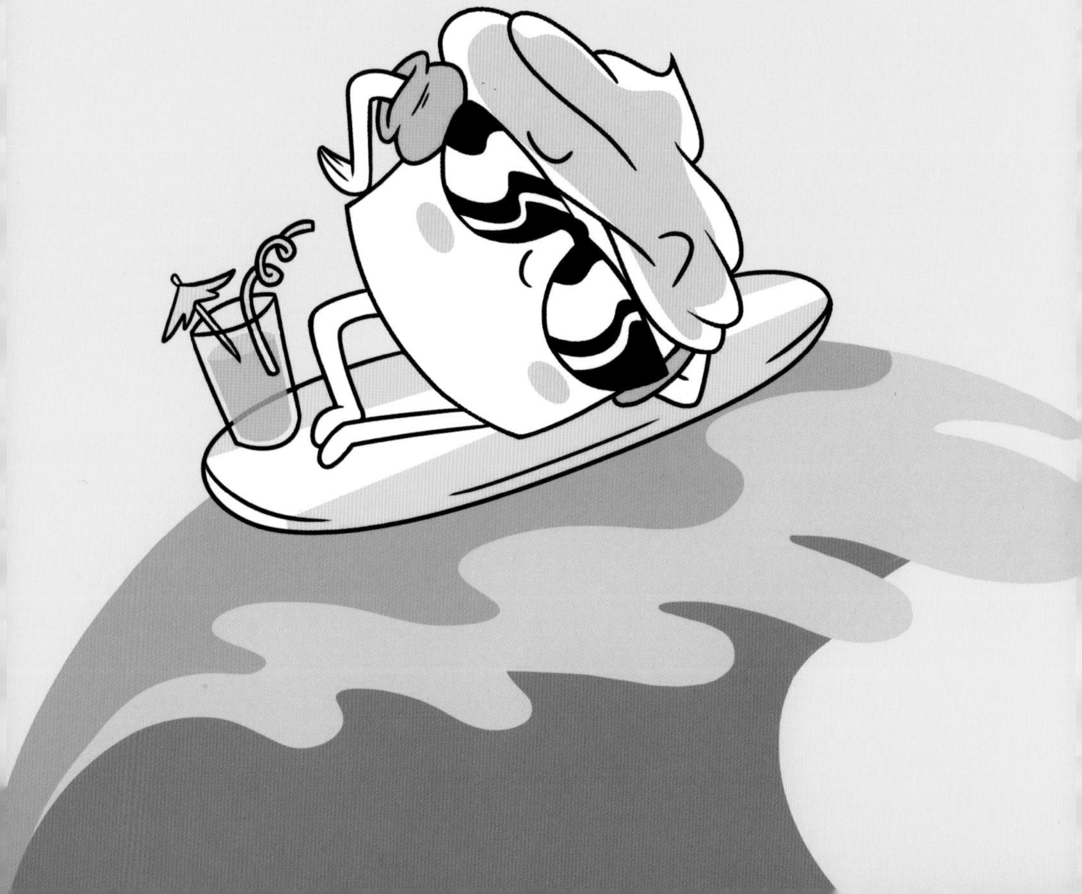

HAPPINESS: RIDE THE WAVE

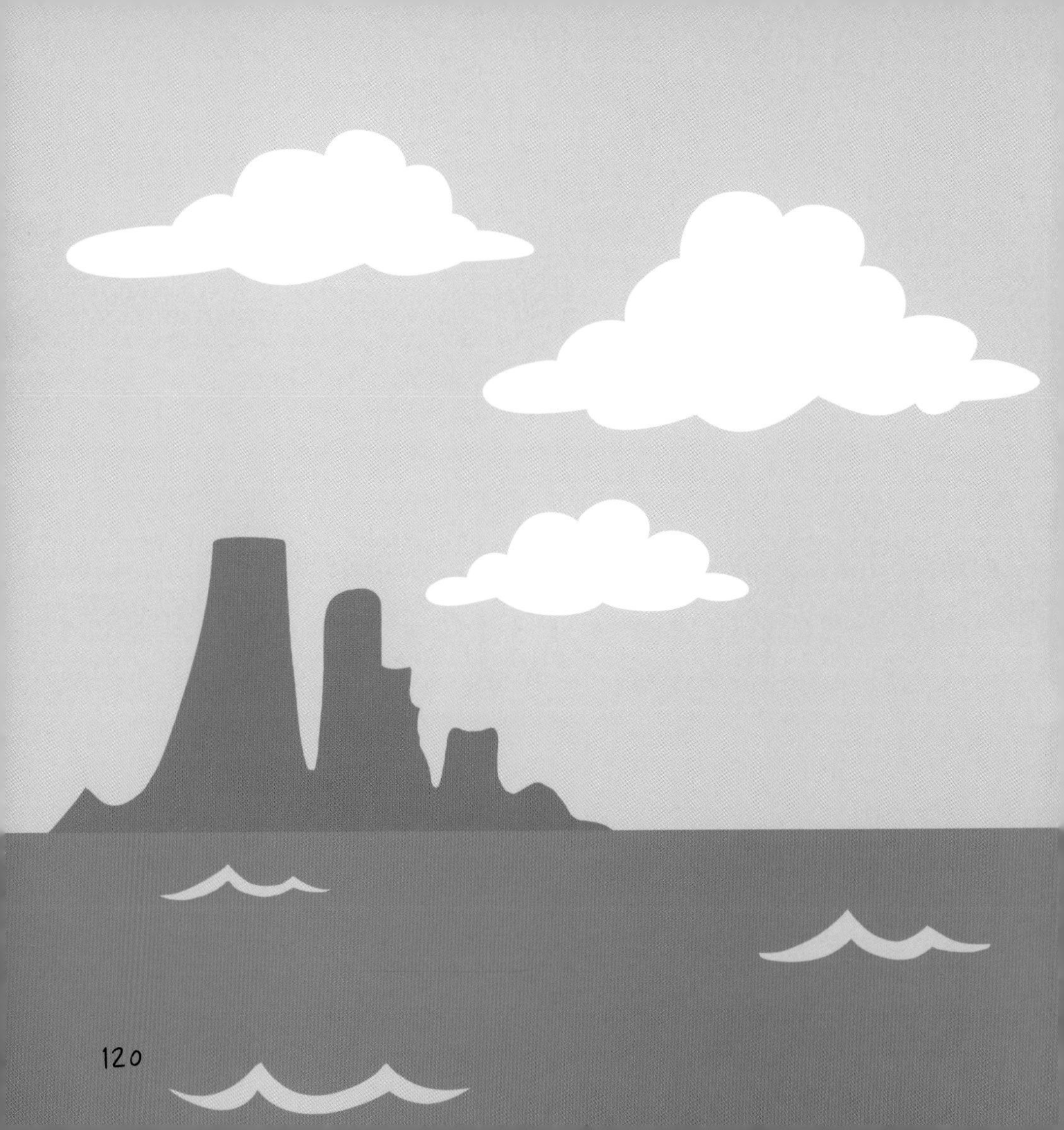

EMOTIONS ARE LIKE A LARGE BODY OF WATER.

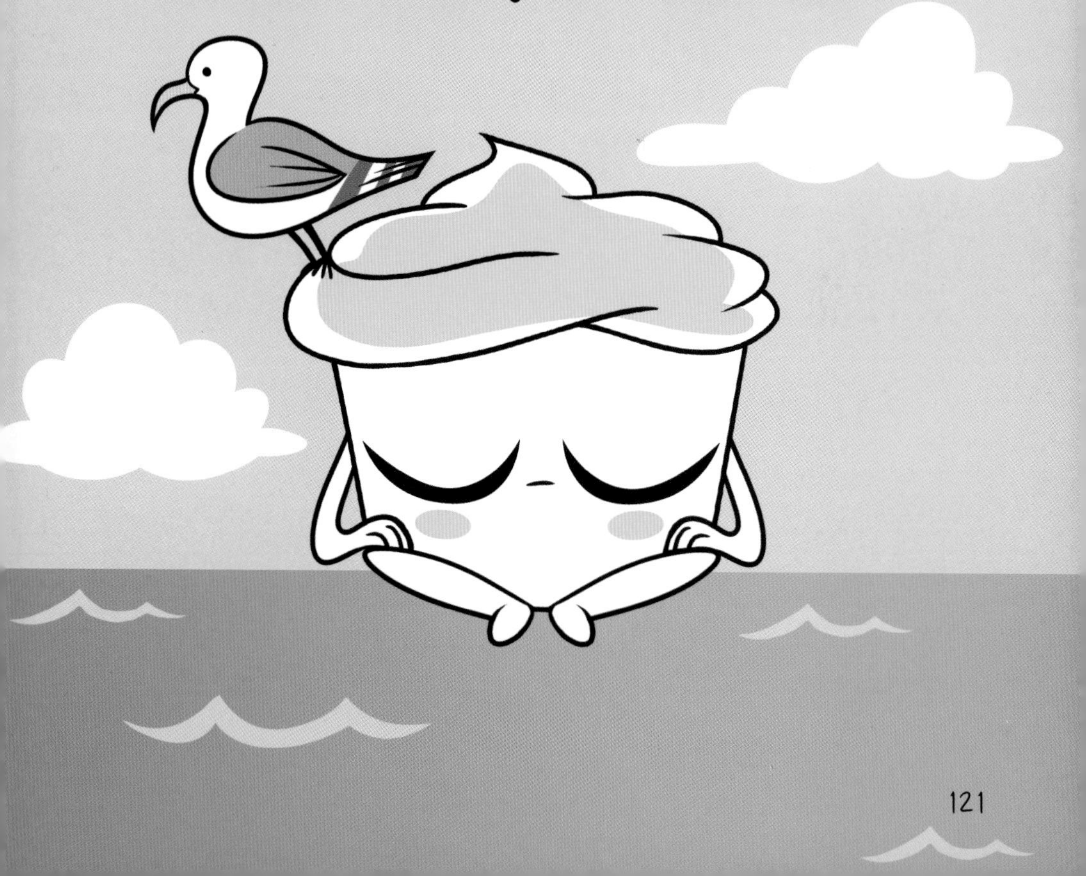

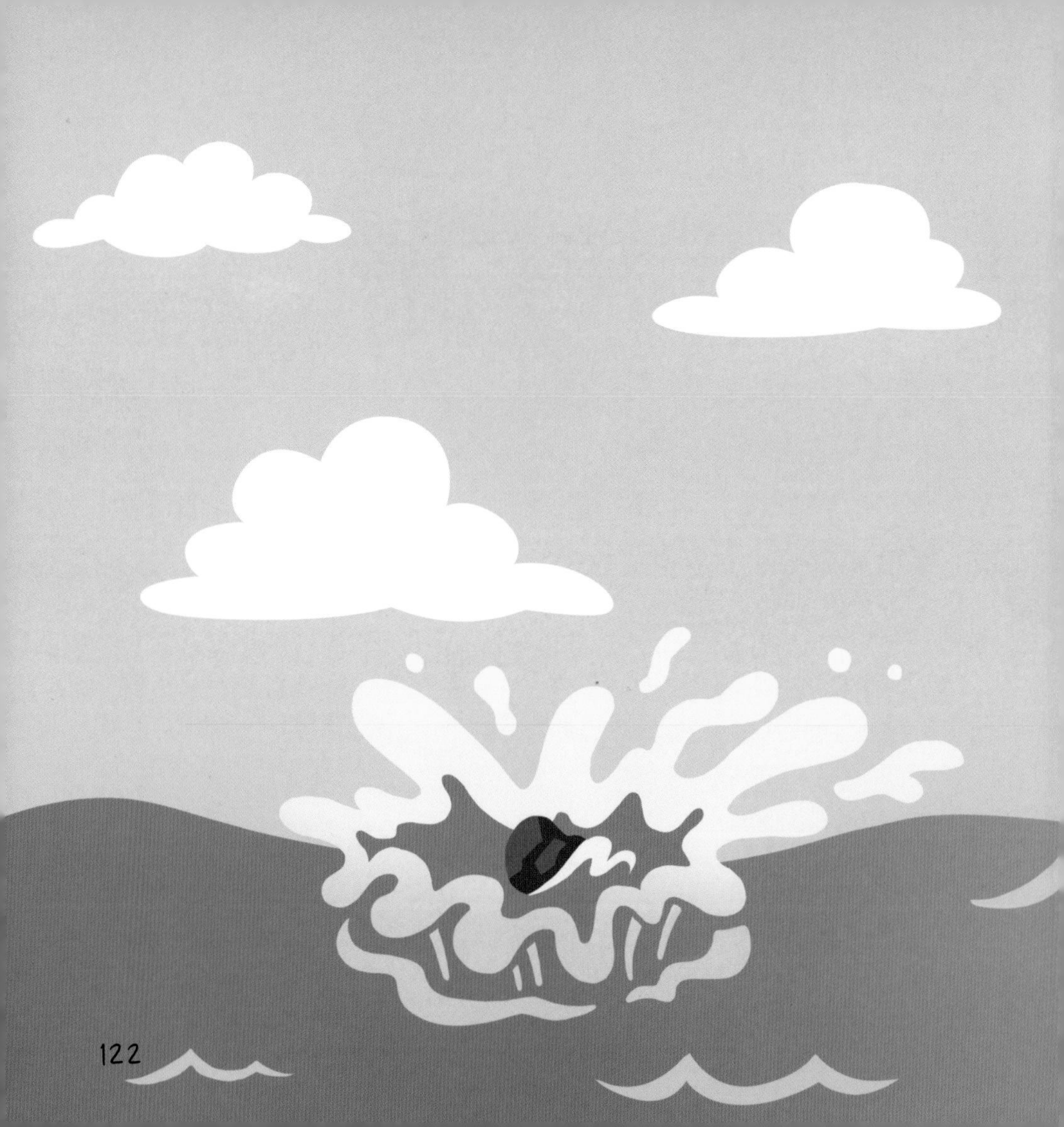

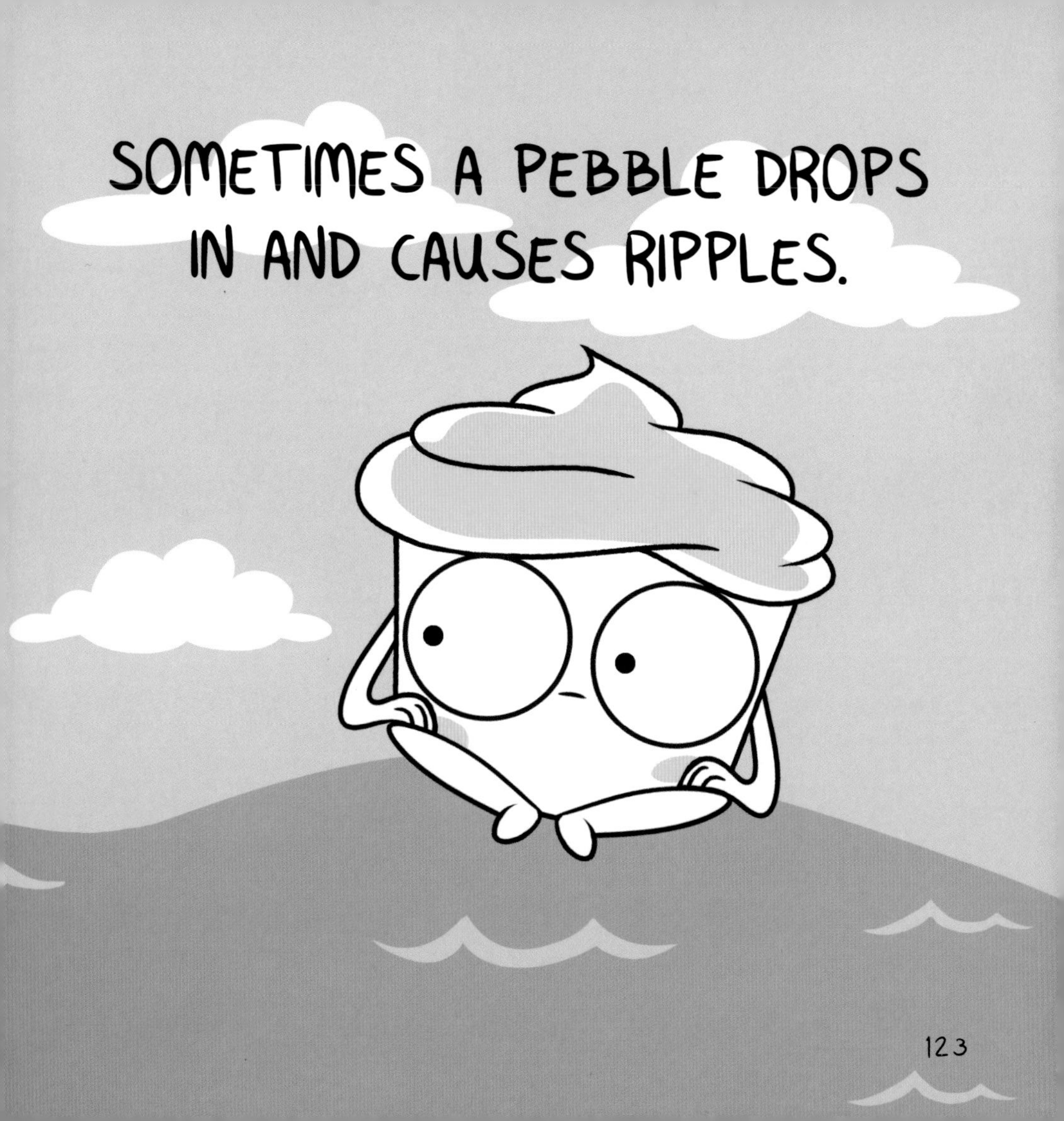
SOMETIMES A PEBBLE DROPS IN AND CAUSES RIPPLES.

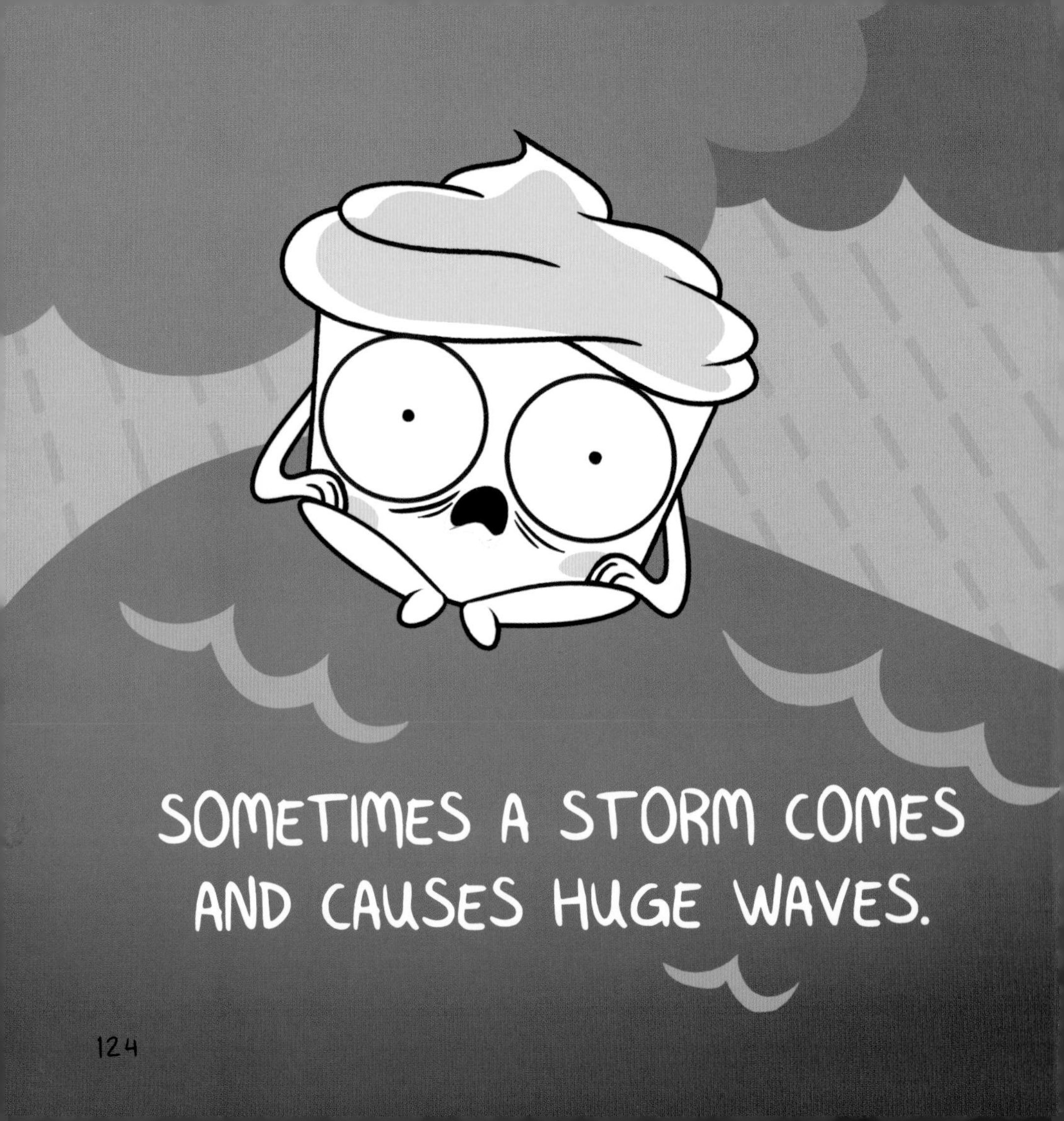

SOMETIMES A STORM COMES
AND CAUSES HUGE WAVES.

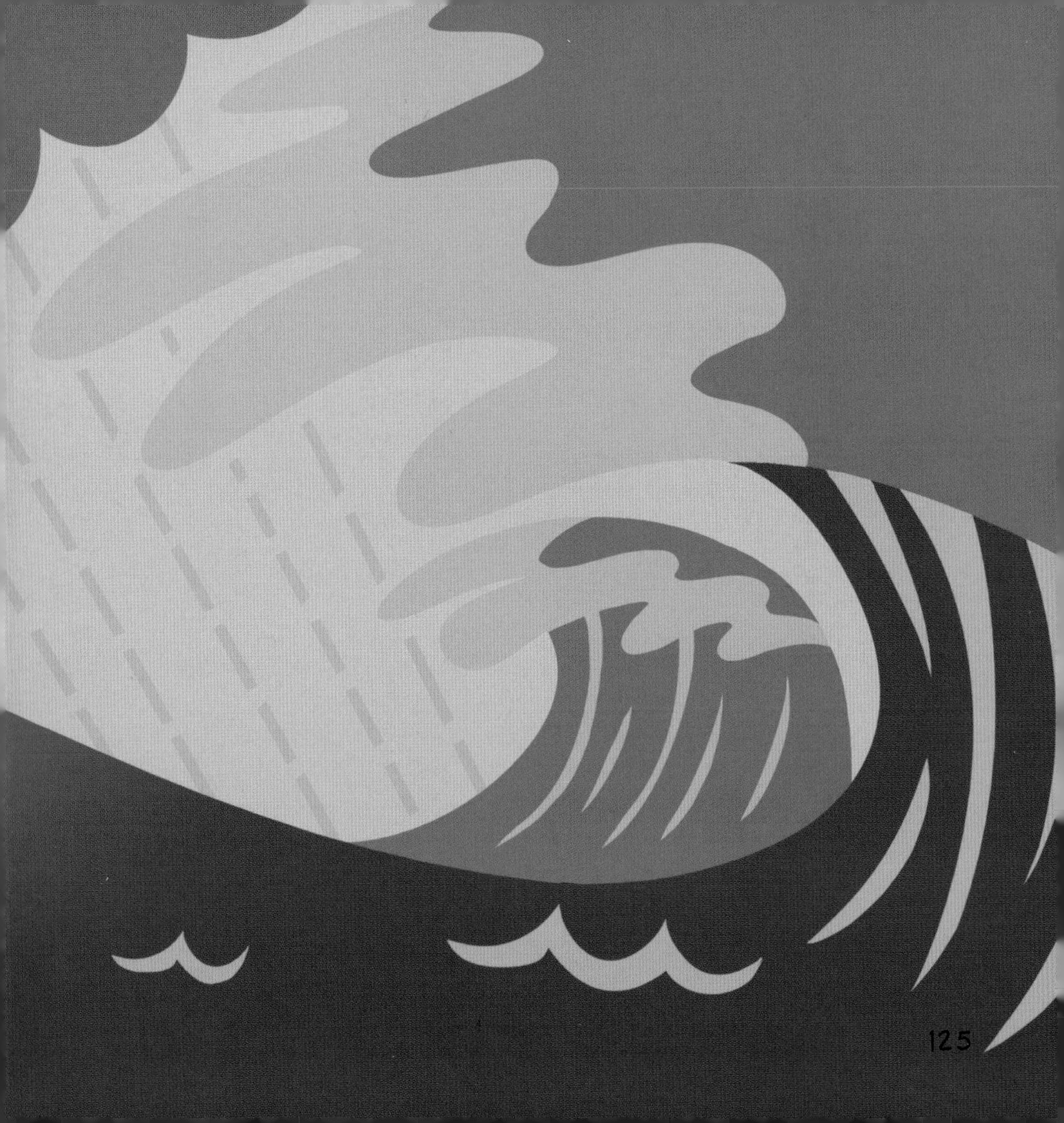

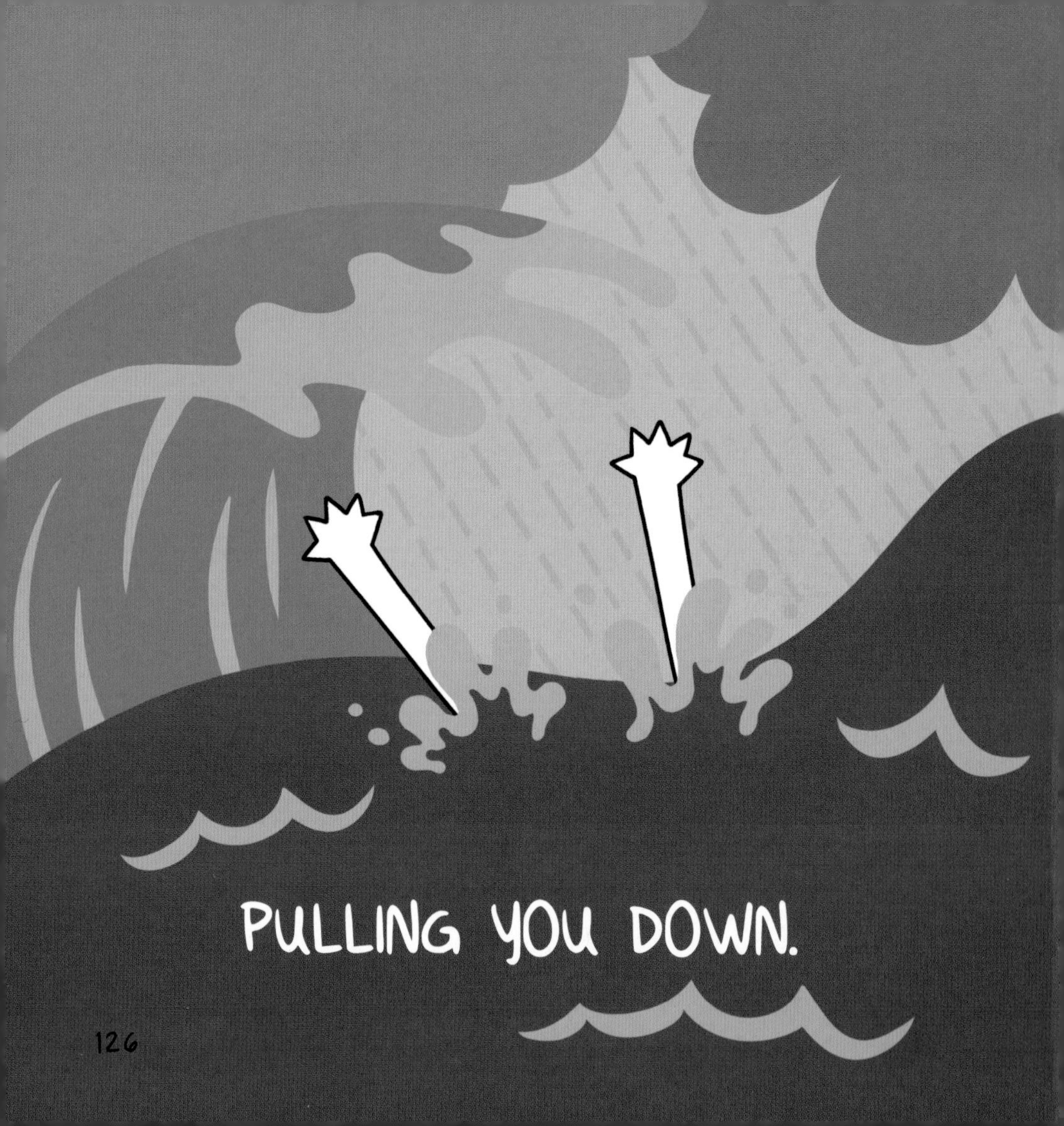
PULLING YOU DOWN.

IF YOU DON'T LET YOURSELF GO WITH THE FLOW AND FEEL WHAT YOU NEED TO FEEL, YOU'LL GET STUCK UNDER WATER.

IT'S OK TO BE SAD SOMETIMES.

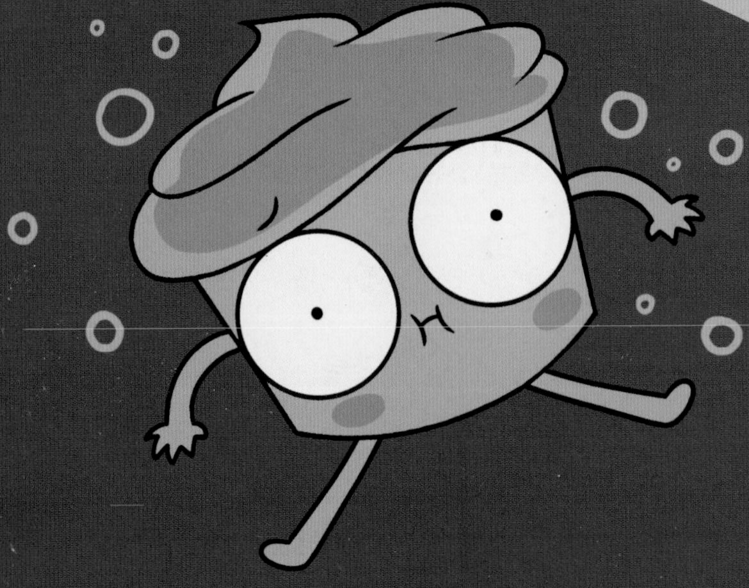